What I Believe

What I Believe
A Collection of My Syndicated Columns

Ben Carson

Creators Publishing
Hermosa Beach, CA

What I Believe
A Collection of My Syndicated Column
Copyright © 2015 Creators Publishing

FIRST EDITION
Creators Publishing
737 3rd St
Hermosa Beach, California 90254
1-310-337-7003
ISBN 978-1-942448-33-4
CREATORS PUBLISHING

CONTENTS

A Note From the Publisher

You don't have to be a brain surgeon to recognize that Ben Carson is an extraordinary person. He grew up in poverty in a single-parent home in inner-city Detroit and, by the age of 33, was the director of pediatric neurosurgery at Johns Hopkins Hospital.

In 2001, he was named by CNN and Time magazine as one of the nation's 20 foremost physicians and scientists, and he was selected by the Library of Congress as one of 89 "Living Legends." The NAACP gave Dr. Carson its highest honor, the Spingarn Medal, and he was awarded the Presidential Medal of Freedom in 2008. His life story was told in the television movie "Gifted Hands," starring Cuba Gooding Jr.

Ben Carson attracted attention during the 2013 National Prayer Breakfast when he questioned the country's tax and health care policies. He did so with President Barack Obama sitting a few feet away on the dais. You can see this speech on YouTube, and you can see how effective Dr. Carson was, particularly because of his calm and understated delivery. Some critics have said that President Obama was upset by the speech, but the president joined with the audience in giving Dr. Carson a standing ovation. I'm not sure if any other Republican presidential candidate has received a standing ovation from Barack Obama.

After that speech, Dr. Carson told a television interviewer that the White House had requested an advance copy of his remarks, but he was unable to provide one because he spoke impromptu, from the heart -- without notes, a teleprompter or any sort of prepared remarks.

When he started writing a weekly column for The Washington Times, Creators jumped at the opportunity to syndicate Ben Carson nationally. Creators is the parent company of Creators Syndicate and Creators Publishing, and we have looked for exciting and controversial figures to syndicate since the company's founding in 1987. We have syndicated other individuals who became presidential candidates, including Democrat Hillary Clinton, Republican Dan Quayle and Reform Party candidate Pat Buchanan.

Ben Carson's columns were read by millions, and we are proud to offer them in this book. We are presenting them in chronological order from the time he wrote each column, beginning in January 2014. By mutual agreement, we have temporarily suspended Dr. Carson's syndicated column because he is an active presidential candidate, but we plan to resume syndicating his column when he is no longer running for or serving as president of the United States.

Rick Newcombe
Creators Publishing

~~~

Thinking for Ourselves: The Rewards of Independence and Common Sense Are Many

January 3, 2014

Earlier this year, one of the mainstream media networks was planning to do a special on my retirement from neurosurgery. They recorded a lecture I gave at my medical school, as well as one given at a high school in Detroit. They also accompanied me to my old stomping grounds, where many of the neighbors came out to greet me and talk about old times.

I was struck by some of their comments, including the notion that I always had lofty, unrealistic dreams, but that they would enjoy hearing about them anyway. Someone else told me that people would always murmur among themselves when I approached, "Here comes Mr. Know-It-All. Let's get out of here." While the network decided not to air the special for some reason unknown to me, it was still a valuable opportunity for me to catch up with old acquaintances.

Similarly, some years ago, I attended the 25th reunion of my high school graduating class. The thing that struck me the most was that many of the "really cool" guys were dead. Many of my other classmates told me how proud they were of my accomplishments and asked me if I remembered how they used to encourage me. Of course I did not -- no such encouragement took place -- but people's memories tend to change over time.

Many of my fellow members of the Horatio Alger Society of Distinguished Americans have recounted similar stories of being regarded as different and not always being part of the "in" crowd when they were growing up. The Horatio Alger Society inducts 10 to 12 new members each year. These are people who grew up under very difficult circumstances and went on to achieve at the highest levels of their respective endeavors. Many of their names would be quite familiar to the public. Are their stories aberrant, or are we truly the captains of our own destiny?

In the game of chess, pawns are just used for the purposes of the royal pieces. In real life, many in power selfishly use "pawns" -- average citizens -- while at the same time vociferously proclaiming that they are the only ones looking out for the interests of the pawns, who happily follow their commands, thinking that this "royal" contingent has their interests in mind. However, in a chess game, a pawn can become any one of the royal pieces, if it can make it to the other side of the board. The opponent will do almost anything to keep one from reaching its goal, because that would interfere with the power structure. If they can keep the pawns on their side of the board, where it is much safer, the status quo can be maintained.

Although no analogy is perfect, it is pretty easy to see the point here. By keeping large groups of Americans complacent and afraid of challenging authority, the position, wealth and status of those in power is secure. The last thing they want is for independent-thinking citizens to realize that this country was designed for them and not for an arrogant ruling class. They dread the possibility of people scrutinizing their words and deeds, and holding them accountable for the same. By using strong-arm tactics and a sheepishly compliant news media, the supposed guardians of truth, they have become very successful at pawn control.

I can't remember how many times during my medical career I was told, "You can't do that; no one has done that before" or "Do you think all the incredibly bright people who have preceded you didn't think of that?" Certainly, if I had listened to those comments instead of critically analyzing the problems and using the triumphs and mistakes of others to produce innovative solutions, my career path would have been considerably different. We have these magnificent brains with outstanding reasoning ability in order to be creative and to critically analyze what we hear and see. We must stop acting like pawns and start acting like masters of our own destiny.

We should not listen to those who say there is too much corruption for honesty and common sense to succeed. We cannot believe that our enemies are too powerful to combat, and we should not accept that the media will never change back to being stalwarts of integrity and truth. We can play the role of nice little pawn or we can be smart, courageous and move out of our comfort zone to accomplish something truly great for our future. It might be a lonely journey at first, but eventually others will see the light. We will shed the pawn mentality and be promoted to the position of proud and independent citizens of America.

~~~

Gray Matter, the Stuff That Really Matters

January 10, 2014

A few years ago, I was participating in a national radio interview when the questioner asked me, "Dr. Carson, I notice that you don't speak very often about race. Why is that?" I replied, "It's because I'm a neurosurgeon."

The puzzled look on her face demanded further clarification.

I proceeded to explain that when I take a patient to the operating room and open the cranium, exposing the brain, I am operating on the actual thing that makes that person who they are. The hair, scalp and skull bones are merely external coverings of the critical entity -- the brain -- that determines all of the most important things about us as human beings. We have a choice of concentrating on superficial characteristics, which mean little or nothing, or concentrating on the source of our humanity, our intellect, our personality and the content of our character.

A few weeks ago, during her television program on the Fox News Channel, Megyn Kelly made reference to the racial makeup of Jesus Christ and Santa Claus. She indicated that in American culture they are usually portrayed as Caucasian. This ignited a firestorm of protests and disagreement, as do many innocent remarks in today's hypersensitive culture. There was little discussion of who Jesus Christ was or his message, nor was there much reference to the symbolism of Santa Claus. Instead, accusations of racist tendencies were leveled.

In the Bible, many characters are described in some detail when it is relevant to the story being told. The fact that there is little or nothing describing the physical appearance of Jesus should serve as an indicator of the irrelevance of racial descriptions for someone with such an important mission.

Why do we in America, almost half a century after the death of Martin Luther King, still continue to make judgments based on the color of one's skin rather than the content of one's character? Those who seem most concerned about race are the so-called "progressives," some of whom claim that if we stop fanning the flames of racial injustice, we will return to the days when racial prejudice was acceptable.

This kind of pessimism is unwarranted, and we need to remember that a great deal of the racism of the past was based on total ignorance, which bred fear and hatred. Those wishing to maintain the unjust status quo were in no hurry to allow the truth to be revealed to whites or blacks about the other side, because such revelations would dispel myths and foster harmony. Thus, segregation and blissful ignorance were maintained at all costs. The fear and loathing that characterize the political atmosphere in America today are also based on ignorance.

Too many people are willing to listen to the inflammatory rhetoric of the dividers who happily toss out accusations of racism against critics of the president of the United States whenever they disagree with his policies. Rather than acting like third-graders and calling each other names, why not actually discuss the policies themselves? Why not have a discussion about the gigantic issues facing our society, such as whether we want the government to control our lives and the lives of everyone around us, as opposed to the original vision for this country of individual independence and self-determination?

Many do not want such discussions to take place, because people will be forced to actually think about their true beliefs, rather than being manipulated for the political purposes of others. If we are to thrive, we must be able to see the big-picture issues and not get bogged down with superficial, peripheral problems. The direction of our country is a very big deal, and if we don't have a serious discussion about it, the nature of our society will change by default.

I am very grateful that God gave us racial variety. Who would want to go to the Smithsonian's National Zoo if every animal were a Thomson's gazelle? Who would visit the national aquarium if every fish were a goldfish? Who would want to get up in the morning if everybody looked exactly like them?

In an episode of "The Twilight Zone" many years ago, a very beautiful and smart young woman was regarded as unsuitable for society. It was revealed at the end of the episode that everyone else was quite ugly, which, for that society, was the norm. They judged the woman harshly because her external appearance was different. Obviously, creator Rod Serling was ahead of his time with his social commentary.

Maybe 2014 will mark a new beginning, a time when we stop judging people based on superficial characteristics. We will know that America has made substantial social progress when black Americans are not expected to adhere to any particular political philosophy, just as white Americans do not have a prescribed political doctrine to which they must adhere. Fortunately, we get to choose whether we are going to use the magnificent gray matter that sits between our ears -- as opposed to our skin color -- to determine who we are and our course of action.

~~~

To Counter Coarseness, Choose Civility

January 15, 2014

As a youngster, I remember being taught to offer my seat on the bus to any elderly person. It was not unusual to see people offering to help carry a heavy or awkward box when a perfect stranger was obviously struggling with one.

In today's culture, it would not be unusual for the stranger to encounter harsh criticism instead of help because he failed to appropriately plan the transport of the heavy box. What has produced the coarsening of attitudes in modern society? Are the crude and mean-spirited comments heard on television and read in the print media having an undesirable effect on the populace at large?

I believe the key to civility is thinking about others first. When we think only about what makes us feel or look good, it becomes easier to disregard the needs and feelings of others.

Prior to the severe economic downturn in 2008, a number of selfish, greedy business types, with complicity from public officials, created schemes to entice relatively inexperienced people to purchase houses that significantly ignored the old, established rule of never taking out a mortgage that was more than two and a half times one's annual salary. These and other variations on paper-pushing manipulations by a small but influential segment of Wall Street types and politicians created enormous fortunes for many who actually produced little or nothing of value.

I do not in any way resent great wealth, and in fact, I greatly admire many of my fellow Americans who through their creativity and dedicated hard work have made contributions that are valuable to many while enriching themselves. That is what capitalism is about. However, when people practice deceit and use clever tactics to enrich themselves or pass legislation at the expense of others, admiration quickly morphs into disgust. Other than Bernie Madoff and a few notable others, not many of these greedy individuals suffered any consequences for their part in the near destruction of our economy and the shattering of the dreams of millions of Americans.

Is it possible that during their formative years, these unethical and uncaring individuals were also influenced by the mean-spirited and self-centered behavior of those in the media or in the political scene who were held in high esteem while practicing mean and deceitful behavior? I am not saying that lack of civility is the root cause of all evil in our society, but I am saying that it can have a profound effect on our feelings toward others and their feelings toward us. Civility and political correctness, contrary to the thinking of many, are not the same. Civility constrains behavior and words based on genuine caring about others, while political correctness is only a facade of caring while hoping to cultivate public approval.

Much politically correct behavior bears no resemblance to logic and common sense. For instance, there was a recent, widely publicized case of a 6-year-old boy in Colorado who was suspended from school for kissing the hand of a classmate. He was initially charged with sexual abuse, but after the public outcry, the charges were downgraded. Many people in the scientific community know that the human brain continues to mature and develop until about age 18. Immature children such as this little boy generally don't even know what sexual abuse is.

Teachers are forced into the role of political-correctness police by bureaucratic administrators who, in many cases, obviously have no sense of the psychological makeup of young children. The potential to do harm to little children with administrative acts of this level of stupidity is tremendous. If we continue down this road of absurdity, we will produce a generation of paranoid and dysfunctional individuals who eventually will be in charge of taking care of those of us who are imposing these rules of political correctness upon them today.

Civility and honesty are highly desirable traits, which should be imparted to our children both through example and planned lessons. This teaching should begin in the home, but certainly teachers, school administrators and other responsible adults should take every opportunity to facilitate the learning process. On the other hand, we must not fall into the trap of being so concerned about innocent words and deeds that we destroy people while worshiping ill-conceived rules of speech and behavior.

It is unreasonable to expect a civil and compassionate society to emerge from a culture that tolerates and often even encourages cruel and dishonest behavior from its leading commentators and leaders. I do not believe these people are capable of seeing fault within themselves. Blinded by their ideology, they are incapable of seeing things from the view of others.

Those of us who can still recognize imperfections in everyone, including ourselves, must not give up on decency, values and the godly principles of loving one's neighbor and developing one's God-given talents to the utmost. They must strive to become valuable to the people around them and have principles that govern their lives. This has nothing to do with political parties, but everything to do with the future of our nation.

~~~

MLK Would Be Alarmed by Black-on-Black Violence

January 16, 2014

It is hard to believe that 50 years have elapsed since Dr. Martin Luther King Jr.'s famous "I Have a Dream" speech on the National Mall in Washington. D.C. I was an 11-year-old child in Detroit languishing in the midst of poverty, but very interested in the strides that were being made in the civil rights movement.

I was the only black kid in my seventh-grade class and over the previous two years had risen from the bottom of the class to the top. My mother forced us to read, which had a profound effect on my brother, Curtis, and me. I was quite optimistic that things were getting better for black people in America.

If King could be resurrected and see what was going on in America today, I suspect he would be extraordinarily pleased by many of the things he observed and disappointed by others. He, like almost everyone else, would be thrilled to know that there is a two-term black president of the United States of America and a black attorney general, as well as many other high government officials, business executives and university presidents.

Perhaps just as thrilling would be the sight of black doctors, lawyers, airline pilots, construction foremen, news anchors, school superintendents and almost any other position imaginable in America. The fact that seeing blacks in such positions no longer raises eyebrows is a testimony to the tremendous progress that has been made in America over the past 50 years.

There are some areas, however, where I suspect he might be less than thrilled. The epidemic of black-on-black violent crime indicates that there has been a significant deterioration of values in the black community. Not only are the lives of their fellow blacks and others being devalued by street thugs, but the lives of unborn babies are being destroyed in disproportionate numbers in the black community.

There was a time when blacks were justifiably angry that the larger community discounted their value, but now, ironically, many members of the black community place little or no value on these precious lives that are snuffed out without thought. I think King would be waging a crusade against the marginalization of black lives in America.

Another area of great concern would be the fact that 73 percent of black babies are born out of wedlock. When this occurs, in most cases, the educational pursuits of the mothers are terminated, and the babies are condemned to a life of poverty and deprivation, which makes them more likely to end up in the penal system or the welfare system. This is a burden not only for the black community, but also for the nation at large.

Although I believe King would be very concerned for all parties in these tragedies, his energies primarily would be channeled into an attempt to give these young women the kind of self-esteem that would preclude their yielding to the charms of individuals who really don't care about them and are only interested in their selfish pleasures.

King was a huge advocate of education and would be horrified by the high dropout rates in many inner-city high schools. He, like many others, was vilified, beaten and jailed for trying to open the doors of education to everyone, regardless of their race.

If he were alive today, he would have to witness people turning their backs on those open doors and choosing to pursue lives of crime or dependency. I do not believe he would simply complain about these things, however. Rather, he would be raising funds to create programs that would show these young people that they do have real choices that could greatly enhance the quality of their lives.

Perhaps the biggest disappointment for King would be the wholesale adoption of a victim mentality that makes people feel that they are entitled to being cared for by others rather than working tirelessly to create wealth and opportunities for their progeny.

The amount of wealth that resides within the black community today is staggering. If the black community, like Jewish, Korean and other cultures in America, learned how to turn over dollars within their own community at least a couple of times before sending them out into the larger society, they would create wealth.

I believe King would advocate such economic policies and would encourage those who benefit from the wealth to reach back and pull others up by providing jobs and opportunities. I think he would stress the fact that this kind of philosophy would foster freedom and independence for the black community, regardless of whether anybody else helps or not.

Finally, we all should remember the aspect of his dream in which he desired that people be judged by their character and not by the color of their skin. In part, this means no one should assume that a black person would adhere to certain political orthodoxy any more so than a white person would.

Certainly, we have come a long way, but there is no room for complacency.

~~~

Allowing American Creativity To Flourish

January 17, 2014

When government grows too large, dependency replaces achievement.

When I was in high school in Detroit, I had a job as a biology laboratory assistant. I spent a substantial amount of time in the greenhouse preparing botany experiments. I had acquired some seeds of an interesting plant and was anxious to use them to produce my own crop of these plants. I planted the seeds in a special container and kept enriching the soil and providing plenty of moisture and sunlight to enhance and accelerate the growth. I was very disappointed with the results and eventually abandoned the project, leaving the seeds in some soil behind the greenhouse to fend for themselves.

To my surprise, one day when I was behind the greenhouse, I discovered that the seeds not only had germinated, but had produced a substantial crop without my help.

I realize that no analogy is perfect and that many people will try to discredit this one, but in this case, I believe the seed is similar to America when it was a fledgling group of colonies. Many people came to America from other countries because they saw an opportunity to lead the life of their choice without a lot of interference from an overarching governing structure.

Although there has been constant tension between those desiring a strong central government that maintains control and order and those desiring maximum personal freedom as long as the rights of others are preserved, our country managed to thrive for many decades with an unprecedented level of autonomy for its citizens. People largely were left to their own devices and could experience great financial success or profound failure without the government playing a major role, other than ensuring the rights of the citizens to pursue their dreams.

Government plays a vital role in the smooth functioning of a successful society. In our country, it was intended that the central government would provide such services as policing, military protection, roads, sanitation, public safety and similar things. In recent years, well-meaning government officials from both parties have determined that citizens need to be more closely managed because they are not capable of acting responsibly or planning for the future. Unfortunately, many of our citizens have grown accustomed to having others regulate their lives and now take little responsibility for their own well-being and that of their families.

In the meantime, the government continues to grow at a rapid pace in order to meet the needs and expectations of the growing dependent class of citizens. This scenario is well known to historians, who realize that bureaucracy begets more bureaucracy. It is incredibly rare -- if not unheard of -- for bureaucratic agencies to conclude that they have grown too big and need to be reduced.

It's not that people who work in the government are bad people; rather, there is a natural tendency for government to grow. Our Founders feared this, and they included measures that we are now ignoring to restrain the growth and power of the central government. Just as I was meddling with the natural growth of those seeds, constant interference in Americans' business by government stifles economic growth, creativity and entrepreneurship. The early settlers of this country had very limited government support, and yet prosperous towns sprang up all over the country. In many cases, entrepreneurs became very wealthy, and that wealth begat wealth and opportunities for others.

Both free enterprise and government want to grow. The free-enterprise system creates wealth and grows the economy, but it is hindered when it is constantly manipulated by government interference and, I dare say, predation. Government growth saps the lifeblood of an expanding economy: money. It is like a spider sucking dry a fly caught in its web, getting ever bigger and requiring more victims to sustain its growth.

If, instead of regulating and taxing to death the engine of growth, our government suddenly decided to leave it alone and allow it to be nourished by free-market forces, like the seed, it would explode with vibrant growth, jobs would return quickly, and to the pleasant surprise of the government, its own coffers would fill because the tax base would be broadened. As an added bonus, the obligations of the government would lessen because there would be fewer citizens on the dole. This would make it possible to reduce and eventually eliminate the national debt. If our government could learn to create a nourishing environment for entrepreneurial endeavors rather than gorging itself on the fruits of their labor, a win-win situation would ensue.

We have strayed far from the idea of independent life and personal responsibility for our populace. Many of our young people cannot even conceive of a world in which personal freedom reigns supreme. This does not mean we should not try to recapture the spirit of freedom and courage that characterized our rapid ascent to the pinnacle of world power.

We the people must control the government before it attains the size and power that will preclude that possibility. It is time we begin discussing with friends, associates and neighbors our vision for our nation and how to realize it. This is not a Democratic or Republican issue. It is an issue of freedom in America for everyone and our progeny.

~~~

A Physician's View on the Sanctity of Life

January 22, 2014

Several years ago, I was consulted by a young woman who was 33 weeks pregnant and was on her way to Kansas to get an abortion. I informed her of the multiple options available to her outside of abortion, and she decided to go through with the pregnancy even though the child had hydrocephalus and would require neurosurgical intervention a few weeks after birth. She kept the baby and loves the beautiful child that has resulted.

A couple of decades ago, I came into the pediatric intensive care unit on morning rounds and was told about a 4-year-old girl who had been hit by an ice-cream truck and was comatose and exhibiting little neurological function other than reactive pupils. I tested her pupillary reflexes, and both pupils were fixed and dilated. The staff indicated to me that this was something that must have just occurred. I grabbed the bed and, with some help, transported her quickly to the operating room for an emergency craniotomy. I was met along the way by a senior neurosurgeon who told me I was wasting my time and that, at best, we would end up with someone in a vegetative state.

Nevertheless, we completed the operation, and a few days later, her pupils became reactive, and she eventually left the hospital. I saw her a few years ago walking through the hospital with her own 4-year-old little girl. She was neurologically fully intact and told me she had become somewhat of a celebrity because of the experience I just related.

What do these two stories have in common? They both involve precious lives that easily could have been discarded.

My entire professional life has been devoted to saving and enhancing lives. Thus, the thought of abortion for the sake of convenience does not appeal to me. I personally have met several people who told me their mothers had considered abortion but happily decided against it.

Most of us instinctively want to protect helpless creatures and sometimes go to great lengths to do so. The television commercials about abused animals are poignant, and as a society, we sometimes delay or cancel large construction projects to protect an "endangered" insect, amphibian or fish. Yet many of us turn a blind eye to the wanton slaughter of millions of helpless human babies, who are much more sophisticated than some of the other creatures, when nothing is at stake other than the convenience of one or both parents. I am not saying we should abandon our efforts to save baby seals and a host of other animals. I am saying: Shouldn't we consider adding human fetuses and babies to the list?

Watching the human fetus develop is awe-inspiring. In less than three months from conception, the little hands and feet are quite recognizable, and distinct facial features characterize cute but very tiny human beings. From Day One, neurons of the brain are proliferating at a rate that will yield a staggering 100 billion neurons by birth. In a matter of nine months from conception, we have a living, breathing, eating, vocal human being who just two months later is socially interactive.

Some people oppose having pregnant women view ultrasonic pictures of their developing babies because they do not want an emotional bond to develop. Careful, unbiased contemplation, however, might yield the conclusion that such bonding is essential to the survival of mankind. Successful farmers nourish and protect their growing crops, and if conditions threaten their crops, they do what is necessary to protect them. Rather than attack the analogy, think about how much more precious a human life is than a stalk of corn.

It is important to try to understand the emotional state of young women seeking an abortion. Instead of judging and condemning them, we need to provide compassion and support. They need to be provided with easy access to adoption services and information about assistance available to them if they decide to keep the baby. I have visited many warm, inviting facilities around the country that exist solely for the purpose of helping these young women.

It is equally, if not more, important to reach these young women before they become pregnant. Forget about those politically correct people who say all lifestyles are equal, and inform those young women about the true consequences of out-of-wedlock birth for those who are not financially independent. We need to make sure they understand that they can provide a much better life for themselves and their children when they plan ahead and value themselves appropriately.

As a society, we cannot be afraid to discuss important social and moral issues. Our heritage as a nation is built on compassion, forgiveness and understanding. Courage is also vitally important, because those who stand on godly principles and values will be attacked. Attempting to characterize love and compassion for human life as a "war on women" is deceitful and pathetic. We the people must stop allowing ourselves to be manipulated by those with agendas that do not include regard for the sanctity of life.

~~~

The Solution to Income Inequality Is Opportunity, Not Entitlement

January 29, 2014

There has been much discussion about income inequality recently. President Obama seems to think we can make significant progress in eliminating poverty by raising the minimum wage, as his State of the Union address highlighted.

Many hope that through a simple declaration, the poor can be elevated to a higher social status. Such people fail to realize that pay is associated with value -- otherwise, we could just pay everybody $1 million a year and let everybody be rich. In a capitalistic society, those individuals who produce the wherewithal to obtain income tend to be paid quite handsomely, while individuals who don't generate significant income are paid accordingly.

As in any situation that involves human beings, there will be some abuses, but generally speaking, this kind of system works by incentivizing individuals to do the things necessary to enhance their value in the marketplace.

Many in the current administration and their sycophants in the news media are trying to persuade Americans that there is significant improvement in the general economy. But record numbers of people are enrolling in the food-stamp program and receiving various government subsidies. Common sense dictates that if the economy were improving, there would be an accompanying decline in the number of people depending on government supplements.

As a child, I was eyewitness to people who preferred a sedentary, nonproductive life as long as they could collect public assistance. Others, including my mother, from the exact same environment, worked incessantly to try to improve their own lives and those of their children. My mother worked as a domestic in the homes of wealthy people who were generous to her because she was dependable, honest and hardworking.

They also learned about my brother and me, because my mother would share our stellar report cards with them once we had conquered our academic doldrums. As a result, these successful people would send us significant monetary incentives to keep up the good work. One of them even loaned me his luxury convertible for a special occasion.

I was never resentful of the wealthy; I was inspired by their achievements and wanted to achieve at the highest possible levels so I could realize my potential and enjoy a pleasant lifestyle.

Luxury and a comfortable lifestyle are no longer goals of mine; they are byproducts of making myself valuable to society. I recognized after many difficulties in early childhood that the person who has the most to do with what happens to me in life is me. Other people and the environment could not thwart me unless I permitted it. Only my attitude and acceptance of the victim mentality could get in the way.

As an adult, the best thing I can do for young people is to give them hope and opportunity. We all need to realize that by showing them kindness and sharing with them, we can have a significant, positive impact on their lives.

We must, however, go beyond rhetoric and put concrete plans into action to allow people to ascend from the lower socioeconomic levels to the apex of our society based on their hard work and creativity.

We should be thinking about creative ways to fund schools in order to even out the distribution of resources between wealthy and impoverished neighborhoods. Corporations and businesses need to concentrate on mutually beneficial apprenticeships and internships for potential workers in their cities. Courses in basic finance and work ethics should be offered in places where such knowledge would not be redundant. These are constructive things that can be done by "we the people."

This does not mean the government doesn't have an important role to play in promoting economic health. The following Jeffersonian quotation is an excellent definition of good government: "A wise and frugal government, which shall restrain men from injuring one another, shall leave them otherwise free to regulate their own pursuits of industry and improvement, and shall not take from the mouth of labor the bread it has earned. This is the sum of good government."

In other words, protect people and get out of the way. Let's use innovation to create opportunity, instead of using government to suppress it. Once we have a vibrant economy, entitlement reform will be a much easier discussion.

~~~

28

The Enduring Spirit of the Tea Parties

February 5, 2014

The famous Boston Tea Party involved disgruntled colonists who felt unfairly treated by the British Motherland, which was imposing an ever-increasing burden of taxation with little or no input from those being taxed.

The British reasoned that they were offering protection to the colonies, and therefore the taxes were justified.

Because the British Empire was almost continuously expanding and engaging in warfare, a great deal of revenue was required. There appeared to be plentiful natural resources and the capacity to develop them in the New World, and the monarch thought these could provide an endless source of revenue.

There was no consideration of the fact that the colonists worked hard to sustain themselves and also wanted to accumulate enough wealth to provide for their later years and for their families.

Interestingly, the much-maligned tea party of today faces the same concerns as the brave pioneers of old. They are also concerned about government overreach with programs such as Obamacare, unnecessary and unlawful surveillance of citizens, blatant and unchecked abuse by the Internal Revenue Service, and government coverups and media complicity.

Neither the Boston Tea Party's participants nor supporters of the modern tea party objected to paying their fair share of taxes, but both witnessed an incessant escalation of government spending, which was always taken out of their hides.

The concept of cutting back on government expenditures was as foreign to the British as it is to our government today, which provides lip service but no meaningful action.

Why do so many members of the political class go to such great lengths to demonize the tea party?

It is not a sophisticated political organization. It consists of a loosely knit group of American citizens from many backgrounds who are not ready to relinquish the power of the people to the hands of government entities whose interests and values do not seem to coincide with theirs.

I think it is because certain politicians have forgotten that they work for us and not the other way around. These politicians are deeply offended by anyone who would dare challenge their "wisdom" and authority.

Recently, a prominent senator publicly spoke out in favor of efforts to crush groups such as the tea party, which is considered by those like him to be comprised of troublemakers, rather than agents of free speech.

This attitude has not been denounced by the Obama administration, and it is antithetical to the principles of freedom of speech and freedom of expression, which were once regarded as precious in America.

As we approach the elections of 2014 and 2016, the tea party and all other groups who respect the Constitution and our Judeo-Christian heritage should put aside minor differences and issues that could be addressed later and present a united front of common sense to combat forces that wish to fundamentally change America.

These forces will make every attempt to magnify a host of social issues on which legitimate differences will always exist. Our entire social system is people-centric, rather than government-centric.

Those who truly understand this will not fall easy prey to those who wish to distract and divide them on these issues. We who think logically will not be shaken by those who say, "These are not minor issues." We realize that they are simply up to their old tricks in an attempt to maintain their power.

Unfortunately, they do not understand the consequences of their misguided ideological agendas of change. They either have refused to read the history books or have engaged in the rewriting of history. In either case, honest reappraisal will educate them to the fact that governmental dominance does not create productivity and prosperity on behalf of the people.

It is obvious that our God-given rights of life, liberty and the pursuit of happiness are jeopardized in today's environment of overt deceit by high government officials and blatant disregard of our Constitution.

When those in power pick and choose the laws they wish to enforce and grant waivers and exemptions to their favored groups, it is clear we are moving away from the principles of fairness and equality that once characterized our nation.

When the president can change laws with the stroke of his pen or a phone call and not be challenged by the other branches of government or by the media, we are in dire straits.

The central question is this: Do you trust the future of your children and grandchildren to this kind of governing structure? Or do you trust those patriotic citizens who wish to preserve the liberties that were fought for by the early Tea Party patriots and by those in "the greatest generation" who stormed the beaches of Normandy in the face of fierce machine-gun fire?

These modern-day patriots are ordinary citizens who toil day-to-day to provide food, education and safety for our citizens. These are the people who fill the ranks of the tea party. They are not demons; they are defenders of freedom. They are you and me.

~~~

Still One Nation Under God

February 12, 2014

We used to characterize the Soviet Union as a godless, evil empire. Like many societies based on communism or socialism, the Soviets saw fit to minimize the importance of God and, in many cases, wreaked unimaginable persecution on religious people.

Why is faith in God anathema to such states? It's because they need to remove any authority other than themselves as the arbiter of right and wrong.

Interestingly, last year Russian President Vladimir Putin criticized Euro-Atlantic countries, including the United States, of becoming godless and moving away from Christian values. Some may bristle at such an accusation, but when you consider that many Americans are hesitant even to mention God or Jesus in public, there may be some validity to his claim. We also casually have tossed out many of the principles espoused in the Bible and have concluded that there's no authority greater than man himself.

The separation clause of the First Amendment of the U.S. Constitution is inappropriately applied to a host of situations that involve religion. By reinterpreting the law to mean separation of God and state, as opposed to the original intent of keeping the church from having undue influence over state affairs and keeping government from ruling the church, secular progressives have succeeded de facto in redefining part of the Constitution. Such success, however, can only be lasting if "we the people" continue to yield our values and beliefs in order to get along.

A number of years ago, some lawyers approached me to advise that we could not hang our "Think Big" banners in public schools. They claimed the "G" stood for God, and this would be tantamount to government endorsement of religion, which would be contrary to the First Amendment. I countered that the First Amendment also forbids government suppression of religious expression and suggested we pursue this argument at the U.S. Supreme Court.

This may have seemed like a bold and reckless statement, but it wasn't. I knew I would be going to the Supreme Court the next week to receive the Jefferson award and figured I would bring up this issue while I was there. And I did.

Justice Sandra Day O'Connor said we were nowhere near violating the First Amendment and that of course we could put up our banners in a public school without constitutional infringement. In this case, I did not back down in the face of bogus accusations, and we prevailed. We all must have the courage to fight for our beliefs, just as our predecessors fought for our future.

While there is no question that our Judeo-Christian values have taken a hit in recent years, we have not yet reached the point of a totally godless government that sets itself up as the supreme authority and giver of rights. As a nation, we must decide definitively whether we believe in God and godly principles. We must decide whether we revere the Bible and what it means when our elected officials take their oaths of office with one hand upon it. If we do nothing, we allow by default the elimination of God as a central figure in our culture.

As secular progressives try to remove all vestiges of God from our society, let us remember the godly principles of loving our fellow man, caring about our neighborhoods, developing our God-given talents to the utmost so that we become valuable to the people around us, and maintaining high principles that govern our lives. Our Judeo-Christian values led this nation to the pinnacle of the world in record time. If we embrace them, they will keep us there.

While we Americans are giving a cold shoulder to our religious heritage, the Russians are warming to religion. The Russians seem to be gaining prestige and influence throughout the world as we are losing ours. I wonder whether there is a correlation.

There are many well-documented stories about God's intervention on behalf of our country during the War of Independence, but one of my favorites involves the Constitutional Convention in 1787. The delegates could not reach consensus on how the Constitution should be written, and the rancor threatened to destroy the fledgling union.

Benjamin Franklin, who was 81 years old, stood before the entire assembly and reminded them of their frequent prayers during the war against Great Britain. At his suggestion, they knelt and prayed -- and then went on to put together a 16-page document known as the Constitution of the United States, one of the most admired documents in history. From that point forward, congressional sessions were started with prayer.

Second Chronicles 7:14 says, "If my people, which are called by my name, shall humble themselves and pray, and seek my face and turn from their wicked ways, then I will hear from heaven, and I will forgive their sins and will heal their land."

These instructions are clear, and secular progressives will shun them. They may control much of the media, but we should not allow them to control our beliefs.

~~~

Beyond Affirmative Action

February 19, 2014

As a child growing up in Detroit and Boston, I had many opportunities to experience the ugly face of racism and witnessed the devastating toll exacted by its mean-spirited nature.

I was a victim of the racism of low expectations for black children, but in retrospect, I can see that many of those attitudes were based on ignorance. Large numbers of white people actually believed that blacks were intellectually inferior, and there was a host of other inaccurate beliefs that whites held about blacks and that blacks held about whites.

Many of those misperceptions probably would have persisted if measures had not been taken to abolish the separation of the races. One of those measures was affirmative action, which was based on the admirable concept that we should take into consideration inherent difficulties faced by minorities growing up in a racist society.

I believe that I benefited from affirmative action. When I applied to Yale University, I thought my chances of being accepted were favorable only because I was somewhat naive about admissions requirements for a high-powered Ivy League institution.

I graduated third in my high school class rather than at the top, largely because my sophomore year was a total waste after I got caught up in the negative aspects of peer pressure and abandoned my studies for the sake of social acceptance. I had a healthy grade-point average by the time I graduated, and one of the Detroit newspapers printed an article that stated I had the highest SAT scores of any student graduating from the Detroit public schools in 20 years. I was also the city executive officer for the ROTC program and had a long list of extracurricular activities.

In my mind, I was pretty hot stuff. Only after I got to Yale and became cognizant of my classmates' many accomplishments did I realize that the admissions committee had taken a substantial risk on me and that I had been extended special consideration. My early academic experiences were traumatic, and but for the grace of God, I would have flunked out.

Fortunately, I was able to adjust to the academic rigors necessary to qualify for medical school admission at the University of Michigan. Medical school was transformative, and I was subsequently accepted into the selective neurosurgical residency at Johns Hopkins. By that time, no special considerations were expected or needed.

Today, there are many young people from a variety of racial backgrounds who are severely deprived economically and could benefit from the extension of a helping hand in education, employment and other endeavors. Such extra consideration is actually helpful to all of us as a society. For each individual we prevent from going down the path of underachievement, there is one less person who will need support from governmental entitlement programs. More importantly, there is one more person who may make substantial contributions that benefit mankind.

The real question is this: Who should receive extra consideration from a nation that has a tradition of cheering for the underdog? My answer to that question may surprise many, but I don't believe race determines underdog status today. Rather, it is the circumstances of one's life that should be considered.

For example, let's take a child who is a member of a racial minority with parents who are successful professionals who have given their child every imaginable advantage. The child applies to a prestigious university with a 3.95 grade-point average, excellent SAT scores and a great record of community service. This child would obviously be an excellent candidate for admission.

Let's take another child who is white, but whose father is incarcerated and whose mother is an alcoholic. Despite these disadvantages, the child still has a 3.7 grade-point average, very good SAT scores and a resume that includes several low-paying jobs. Without taking any other factors into consideration, the choice is clear: The first student would be admitted over the second.

However, I think extra consideration should go to the second child, who has clearly demonstrated the tenacity and determination to succeed in the face of daunting odds. If that second child happens to be a member of a racial minority, obviously he would receive the extra consideration, as well.

I call this "compassionate action." Such a strategy demonstrates sensitivity and compassion, as well as recognition of substantial achievement in the face of difficult obstacles. The groups who benefit from compassionate action will probably change over time, depending on which ones have the greatest number of obstacles to overcome. The point is, it's time to be more concerned about the content of character than the color of skin when extending extra consideration.

Some people are still willfully ignorant and wish to look at external physical characteristics in determining a person's abilities. These people are unlikely to change even when equipped with information, because they already think they possess superior knowledge and wisdom. All we can do is pray that someday, they will have a change of heart.

~~~

Acting Like a Founder

February 26, 2014

Most of us can remember feeling that someone had done us a great injustice. On those occasions, we want nothing more than to exact revenge. I remember being unfairly treated as a lowly ROTC cadet by one of the sergeants who resented the fact that my brother had been promoted to captain and company commander over him.

I was ambitious and worked extremely hard, resulting in my promotion in record time to the rank of colonel and city executive officer. This individual was now firmly under my command, and I could have wreaked havoc in his life. Instead, I chose to give him extra responsibilities. Responding to the challenge, he proved himself to be quite capable, earning further promotions. Because I resisted the urge to retaliate, we both won. This same principle applies in politics.

Unfortunately, in the past, we have been a reactionary country, resulting in political shifts back and forth from left to right without a lot of forward progress. After attaining power, both sides act in ways that are less than honorable, but they justify their actions by citing similar transgressions performed by the other side. This immature behavior is vividly exhibited by President Obama in his shameless use of executive orders to try to force the eventual success of Obamacare.

Administration supporters defend his strategy by pointing out that previous presidents have issued even more executive orders than Obama. It's like saying that punching someone 40 times is more harmful than shooting him four times. However, it's not the quantity of executive orders that matters, but their impact.

There are always people who attempt to pick apart an analogy, but most readers will see the point. In the current controversy, a massive politically motivated government program was forced on half of the population with their opinions completely disregarded. No legislation of this magnitude ever had been passed in the history of the United States by one party with unanimous opposition by the other party. Each executive order to sustain Obamacare is like pouring salt in a wound. Furthermore, the concept of seeking common ground is further damaged.

When the political pendulum swings again, which I predict will begin this November, it is imperative for the sake of our progeny that those in power act like "the adults in the room" and govern in a lawful and constitutional manner. This means refraining from the use of excessive government interference in choosing winners and losers. It also means an evenhanded enforcement of all of our laws rather than repeating the Obama administration's practice of selective law enforcement. Adult governance is founded upon objectivity, not ideology.

The American people have suffered through decades of power-drunk politicians, many of whom practiced deceitful manipulation. This has caused tens of millions of Americans to abandon in disgust their duty to be informed and responsible voters, which only makes the situation worse.

I have encountered a large number of elderly people who have told me that they have given up on the United States and are simply waiting to die. This is the reason that more eligible voters opted not to vote in the last presidential election than actually voted for either candidate. Many of these people are members of "the greatest generation." They fought tangible and visible forces that threatened our freedom. The forces facing us now are less tangible, but are nevertheless at least as lethal to our way of life.

Despite all the naysayers on both sides, I am convinced by the people I encounter on the speaking circuit that common sense, honesty and fairness can return to the corridors of power in America. We can govern in a manner that not only re-engages millions, but also provides liberty and justice for all.

As it was in the days of the Founding Fathers before the American Revolution, now it is necessary for ordinary Americans to engage their neighbors, friends and colleagues in serious discussions about what kind of nation they want to pass on to their children and grandchildren. It is important that everyone knows who represents them both at the state level and at the national level. The party affiliation of those representatives is not nearly as important as their voting record. Every American, regardless of their political affiliation, must distinguish those who represent the free-enterprise system based on personal responsibility and equal treatment from those who are willing to give away our personal freedom in order to enhance the size and scope of the government.

The power to reverse the deterioration of our nation is within the hands of "we the people." We must realize that our countrymen are not our enemies, and we must understand that we cannot rely on those in the media and in politics to tell us the truth. We need to go beyond them and rely on ourselves to craft a truly free America that works for all of us. This means we must become informed voters and use our votes effectively to choose the kind of leadership that represents the will of the people.

~~~

Uprooting Obamacare with Better Ideas

March 5, 2014

As a child, I was attracted to anything that dealt with medicine. Many stories featured Johns Hopkins Hospital, and eventually I was privileged to spend 36 years at Johns Hopkins working with brilliant and caring colleagues who dedicated their lives to the art and science of healing.

After a storybook career that included thousands of operations and many sleepless nights, I looked forward to retirement, thinking it would be relaxing. However, life throws many curveballs, and sometimes the ordering of our steps is not of our own choosing. I now find myself deeply immersed in trying to heal the health care environment, because if you cure the organism and put it back into a sick environment, you really have not accomplished very much.

Recently, I was giving a speech in Sikeston, Mo., where I had the opportunity to be reacquainted with a 21-year-old man named T.J. He likes to go fishing and play cards with his friends, and to a stranger, he sounds like a pretty regular 20-something. However, T.J. has lived anything but a regular life.

At just 9 months of age, he was diagnosed with an aggressive brain tumor. His mother was told not to expect him to see his second birthday. This is news that no mother should have to hear. After 17 surgeries -- seven of which I performed in a relatively short period of time -- T.J. was finally out of the woods. Through a combination of providence and the marvels of modern medicine, T.J. survived this ordeal, and it was quite an experience to get to see him and his dedicated family again.

I share this story to help explain why I have decided to become chairman of the Save Our Healthcare Project, which was organized by a group called the American Legacy PAC. Our mission is to lead a national citizens' effort to hold Washington accountable, re-center the health care debate around doctors and patients, and begin the process of replacing Obamacare with patient-centered reforms that will allow every American access to the best, most affordable care in the world. If you would like to join us, please visit SaveOurHealthcare.org.

I believe a nationwide effort such as this is vital. As much as I have been privileged to treat people such as T.J., I am but one person -- and both the problems and the solutions to our health care woes are bigger than any one person.

As we move forward, we will seek to underscore two points that have gotten lost in the daily back-and-forth over broken websites, increased premiums and dropped coverage. First, the underlying and unfixable flaw of Obamacare is that it goes against all of the lessons of human history and puts its trust in a centralized bureaucracy instead of free individuals. Second, repealing Obamacare is not an end in itself. Those of us who believe in the Constitution, free enterprise and individual freedom have an absolute responsibility to provide the country with a new and better direction, and that is what we intend to do.

From my experience, I know that nothing is more personal than health care. After all, it's about the health of the people we love and care about. Every step in the direction of centralization is a step away from personalization. I steadfastly believe that no centralized bureaucracy and no politician -- Republican or Democrat -- should ever get in the way of decisions best made by patients, families and doctors.

While we have strong ties that bind us all together, we are a nation of individuals, endowed by our Creator with certain inalienable rights. Each of us has our own needs, and our elected officials must recognize that top-down cookie-cutter solutions simply will not work. Ultimately, they increase costs and decrease freedom of choice.

If such solutions will not work, we must offer ones that will. Every day that the American people are unaware of alternative ideas is a day that Obamacare's roots grow deeper and more permanent.

In direct contrast to the approach of "we have to pass the bill to find out what's in it," which gave us more than 2,700 pages of regulation and confusion, we will work this year to rally the country in a gradual, step-by-step way around a series of positive proposals that people can understand. We will move forward in such a way because I believe ideas matter. I can't begin to thank all of the people who have sent excellent ideas on health care reform.

Those of us who think we can do better than Obamacare cannot hope to win national elections, let alone win a massive policy fight, if we don't first win the argument. The argument about the right path forward for the American health care system is a big argument to win.

I fully expect that as we seek to reform major institutions, I will be attacked by those who disagree. Critics undoubtedly will try to pigeonhole this effort as just another attack on President Obama and his signature legislative achievement. However, this is about much more than Obamacare. It's about helping to ensure that Americans of every background have the opportunity to live longer, happier and more independent lives with more freedom and more choice.

The American people currently are witnessing the failure of centralized government to deliver affordable, quality health care, and there is no better time than this to consider better alternatives. This is a massive undertaking, and it will be tough. But when I look into the eyes of someone such as T.J. in Missouri, I know there are much tougher things to confront in this world.

I also know that if we have courage, then there is hope for a better future.

~~~

The Profligate Path to Servitude

March 12, 2014

As a teenager, I began a new lifelong routine of starting and ending each day reading from the book of Proverbs, which, of course, was written by Solomon, a very wise man. Interestingly, my parents gave me the middle name of Solomon -- not that I claim even a modicum of his wisdom.

After Solomon became the king of Israel, he gained great renown when two women came before him claiming to be the mother of the same infant. Solomon decreed that the baby should be divided and half given to each woman, at which time the real mother immediately relinquished her claim.

This made the judgment quite simple. I believe God has a sense of humor, not only because of my middle name and my affinity for Solomonic proverbs, but because I, too, gained great renown by dividing babies. In my case, it was complexly joined craniopagus twins.

One of the verses that seems pertinent to America today is Proverbs 22:7, which says, "The rich ruleth over the poor, and the borrower is servant to the lender." Most of us grew up hearing that debt is a bad thing. The advent and wide dissemination of credit cards diminished such teachings, and those in charge of our nation's finances over the past few decades seem to revel in debt.

As a nation, we currently are carrying a national debt of $17.5 trillion. If we repaid it at a rate of $10 million per day, seven days a week, 365 days per year, it would take 4,700 years to repay. The only reason that we can sustain such a level of debt is our status as the international reserve currency for the world.

This is a position usually reserved for the most reliable and strongest economic nation, and this status allows us to print money. If Greece could print money, it would not be bankrupt, although it probably would continue to drive up its debt.

Additionally, we have unfunded liabilities of at least $100 trillion.

Why am I concerned about this? I have been talking about this issue since long before Russian President Vladimir Putin's recent threat to abandon the U.S. dollar as Russia's reserve currency. Unless he could attract many other nations to do the same, he likely would inflict more short-term damage on his own country than on the United States.

Nevertheless, the very mention of such an action should send shivers down our spine. He recognizes our vulnerable position, which is exacerbated by our insistence on incurring unsustainable levels of debt. I have no doubt that at a strategic moment, he will exploit our weakness.

A United Nations committee in 2010 recommended a change in world reserve currency policies, and others such as China have made similar suggestions. They are beginning to doubt the stability of America's financial infrastructure.

Our continued fiscal irresponsibility not only threatens the financial well-being of the next generation of Americans, but it also increasingly jeopardizes U.S. security. Our international influence is weakened, as our borrower status makes us vulnerable to threats from Putin and others. Perhaps worst of all, if our status as the world's reserve currency issuer changes, there could be a dramatic decline in our standard of living.

If this occurs, the Occupy Wall Street movement will seem like a walk in the park compared with the civil unrest that will result. It does not require a great imagination to envision some of the freedom-limiting responses that might then occur. Many say this is simply paranoia and fear-mongering, which is what the so-called elites traditionally say before a catastrophic collapse.

The good news is we can do better. However, we the people must first do our homework and make sure we know who our congressional representatives are and how they vote, not how they say they vote. If they are in favor of continued fiscal lunacy, as evidenced by their votes that keep raising our national debt, they need to be replaced by responsible candidates from any party who understand the implications of their actions.

We need people who understand that in order for businesses to grow and prosper the government must remove the heavy boot of regulation and interference from their necks. We need those who realize that taxation is supposed to provide the necessary revenues to operate a government that provides for the safety, infrastructure and freedom of the people.

The purpose of taxation is not to control behavior and certainly not to justify a government takeover of health care that initiated the most massive shift of power from the people to the government in our history. By declaring pertinent parts of the Affordable Care Act a tax, the Supreme Court facilitated the demise of freedom in America.

These should not be partisan issues, but rather the concerns of every freedom-loving American citizen who wishes to see prosperity return to our shores.

Fiscal responsibility, fair taxation, intelligent environmental and energy policies, strong international leadership, evidence-based educational policies, cost-effective health care that is readily available to everyone, and honesty can prevail, but some feathers of those who are currently comfortable may need to be ruffled.

We need to discuss all of these things openly, rather than giving ear to the constant demagoguery that now exists. We must then vote responsibly with full knowledge of records and remain vigilant to preserve freedom and justice for all. We still have the power to craft a better future, but urgency grows.

~~~

The Insidious Effect of Political Correctness

March 19, 2014

When I was in high school in Detroit, there was a great deal of emphasis on clothing. As I became increasingly interested in fitting in with the "in crowd," fashion supplanted academic achievement in my hierarchy of importance. My grades plummeted, and I became a person who was less pleasant and more self-absorbed.

My mother was disappointed because she thought I had enough insight and intelligence to avoid the flypaper trap of acting like everyone else.

Fortunately, after wasting a year pursuing acceptance, I realized that my dreams went far beyond silk shirts and sharkskin pants. I decided to forsake the "in crowd" and redoubled my academic efforts in time to rescue my sinking grade-point average and gain admission to an Ivy League university.

To say that the "in crowd" was disgruntled when I abandoned their association would be a gross understatement. It eventually became clear to them that I would not rejoin their ranks under any circumstances, and they left me alone.

Despite the insults hurled at me, at the time of graduation, my classmates voted me "most likely to succeed." This indicated that they knew the prerequisites for success but were unwilling to fulfill them, and they wanted others to remain shackled to their underachieving lifestyle.

Political correctness (PC) operates in much the same fashion. It is in place to ensure conformity to the prescribed expressions and lifestyles dictated by the elites.

There are rewards of acceptance and praise for members of the "in crowd" as they attempt to silence or destroy any who dare think for themselves or express opposing views. Similarly, the purveyors of PC seize upon a word or phrase, which they emphasize in an attempt to divert attention away from the actual issue that doesn't fit their narrative.

I have stated in the past that Obamacare is the worst thing to occur in our country since slavery. Why did I make such a strong statement? Obviously, I recognize the horrors of slavery. My roots have been traced back to Africa, and I am aware of some horrendous deeds inflicted on my ancestors in this country.

The purpose of the statement was not to minimize the most evil institution in American history, but rather to draw attention to a profound shift of power from the people to the government.

I think this shift is beginning to wrench the nation from one centered on the rights of individual citizens to one that accepts the right of the government to control even the most essential parts of our lives. This strikes a serious blow to the concept of freedom that gave birth to this nation.

Some well-known radicals have publicly written and stated that in order for their idea of a utopian, egalitarian society to emerge in the United States, the government must control health care, which ensures the dependency of the populace on government. Historical analysis of many countries that have gone this route demonstrates the obliteration of the middle class and a massive expansion of the poor, dependent class with a relatively small number of elites in control.

This is sobering information, and those who want to fundamentally change America would much rather demonize someone who is exposing this agenda than engage in a conversation that they cannot win. Others join in the fray, happily marching in lockstep with those who are attempting to convert our nation to something we won't recognize, having no idea that they are being used.

Vladimir Lenin is sometimes credited with coining the phrase "useful idiots" to describe such individuals.

It is time in America for the people to open their eyes to what is happening all around them as our nation undergoes radical changes without so much as a conversation out of fear of being called a name, of facing economically adverse actions or of enduring government harassment, characterized by the perpetrators as "phony scandals."

Political correctness is antithetical to our founding principles of freedom of speech and freedom of expression. Its most powerful tool is intimidation.

If it is not vigorously opposed, its proponents win by default, because the victims adopt a "go along to get along" attitude. Major allies in the imposition of PC are members of the media, some of whom thrive on controversy while others are true ideologues.

The true believers would be amusing if it were not so sad to behold them dissecting, distorting and repeating words in an attempt to divert attention from the rise of government control.

The American people must learn to identify and ignore political correctness if we are to escape the bitter ideological grenades that are destroying our unity and strength. Political correctness is impotent if we the people are fearless. Let us emphasize intelligent discussion of issues and leave the smear campaigns to those with no constructive ideas.

~~~

Energy's Role in the Path to Peace

March 26, 2014

While the media have been focused on the missing Malaysian aircraft, massive alterations of the world's geopolitical terrain are underway simultaneously.

The annexation of Crimea by Russia should not have been a surprise for anyone who suspects that President Vladimir Putin is trying to re-establish a powerful Soviet-style empire. When he aggressively attacked Georgia in 2008 after both Georgia and Ukraine failed to obtain NATO admission at the Bucharest Summit, we should have realized that his goals were not limited to one territory. I suspect he is now calculating an excuse to occupy the easiest regions of Ukraine first and then the whole country over time.

The United States encouraged Ukraine to give up its nuclear arsenal and to de-emphasize its military complex, but in its moment of dire need for tangible support, will we have the courage and fortitude to help stop Russian aggression, which ultimately could lead to another Cold War or worse?

Many probably have forgotten the worldwide turmoil created during the Cold War, which ended a quarter-century ago. Allowing conditions to mature that might re-create another dominant world power hostile toward the United States could easily reinforce those radical elements who wish to see the demise of this nation. One of the ways we permit such conditions to arise is through our fiscal irresponsibility, which substantially weakens us because the borrower is subservient to the lender. Can we be objective in our treatment of nations, no matter what their actions, if we owe them great sums of money?

Ronald Reagan facilitated the demise of the Soviet Union without firing a single shot. He enacted policies that resulted in a financial meltdown that ended the brutal Soviet reign. The recent precipitous fall of the Russian stock market cannot go unnoticed by Putin, and more financial pressure applied immediately could give pause to his grandiose schemes. We could freeze Russian financial assets, downgrade trade associations or rapidly establish energy production policies to free the European Union from the Russian energy stranglehold.

EU energy freedom would require the quick establishment of a rational energy development platform that does not cater to far-left environmentalists. Many advocates of common sense are also concerned about the environment, but are reasonable enough to realize that rather than using Environmental Protection Agency regulations to stifle abundant energy production, we can use the EPA in conjunction with the spirit of innovation and entrepreneurship to produce and export a vast amount of clean energy. This could significantly improve our bargaining position throughout the world.

Whether we are experiencing global warming or a coming ice age, which was predicted in the 1970s, we as responsible human beings must be concerned about our surroundings and what we will pass on to future generations. However, to use climate change as an excuse not to develop our God-given resources makes little sense. Expanding our wealth of energy resources, as well as encouraging the development of new renewable energy sources, would provide an enormous economic lift with obvious benefits, but it also would bolster our role as a formidable player in the struggle for world leadership.

The rapidly changing geopolitical scene cannot successfully be managed by leading from behind. We need to put aside partisan ideological bickering and use our collective knowledge and wisdom to thwart the redevelopment of a powerful and dangerous rival for global influence. Perception is reality, and it is crucial that we not be seen as timid and waffling during the opening moves of this strategic chess match.

Our allies must know that we have their backs when they get into difficult situations, and our support must be pronounced and immediate. If we call upon independent nations such as Ukraine to abandon their most potent weapons of defense and then only lend tepid support when their independence is threatened, we would be foolish to believe that others in the world are not observing our behavior. Consistent reliability and strong support in these matters will lead to strong support when we call upon our allies to join us in employing economic leverage against rogues who threaten world peace.

Americans should be supportive and encouraging of our leaders during times of international crisis, but let's hope they are listening to voices from all major parties about the ramifications of each option available to us in this fight. Let's further hope that they can see the big picture and understand the importance of using all of our resources, including natural energy, to achieve our objectives. Developing our natural energy resources, controlling our national debt, consistently supporting our allies and aggressively opposing our foes without playing politics will help improve our status in the world and make peace more likely. The stakes are too high to simply be reactive. We must act if we are to lead.

~~~

Outwitting the Purveyors of Dependency

April 2, 2014

Divide and conquer is an age-old strategy, effectively used by many in positions of power to ensure that they retain their wealth and authority.

During the dark days of slavery in America, there were many geographic areas where the number of slaves significantly surpassed the number of whites and slave owners. This occasioned appropriate anxiety for the owners, who cleverly sowed seeds of discord among the different groups of slaves in an attempt to effectively destroy unity. For example, field slaves were told that the house slaves thought of themselves as superior.

This worked in most cases, although there were notable instances of secret cooperation between the slaves to accomplish various goals. It required real wisdom and insight to avoid easy manipulation by the slave owners, who usually used slaves loyal to them to accomplish their nefarious objectives.

In today's culture, there are political forces that see the descendants of slaves as useful objects for maintaining their positions of wealth and power. By promising to care for their every need, they create dependency.

Frightening those dependents into thinking they will be abandoned if others are in control, they create loyalty that is undeserved but fierce, loyalty that translates into the real goal: votes. Anything or anyone that threatens this paradigm of victim and protector must be destroyed, lest the victims recognize the deceitfulness of their manipulators and revolt.

The most dangerous people to the modern manipulators are people who have freed themselves from the plantation mentality. They eschew the propaganda of victimhood and advocate for personal responsibility. They see the value found in the true compassion of a hand up rather than a handout.

The tragedy is that many "leaders" of the black community succumb to the poison of the controlling elites, who make them feel "cool" and important. I'm sure that some actually realize what is happening, but -- like the kids you remember in high school -- they don't want to risk being ostracized and expelled from the "in crowd" and therefore remain silent.

It is so important for the black community to realize that there is tremendous strength in unity and that disagreement on some issues does not have to create animosity. In fact, by engaging in open discussions rather than demonizing, a great deal can be learned by all parties.

I am a registered independent, but I have many friends who are Democrats and many who are Republicans. One friend who identifies himself as a Democrat left Alabama at age 16 and headed to Boston in search of employment. He accidentally ended up in Hartford, Conn., and worked in a lowly position as a construction aide for a hotel that was being built. This young black man from Birmingham had a strong work ethic and was gifted with common sense.

Today, he not only owns that hotel, but he also owns many other businesses and is a philanthropist. We do not disagree about most important things, but we have some political disagreements, which have no negative impact on our friendship or our ability to work together on projects. If someone tried to exploit our differences, we would have a hearty laugh at their expense.

Those who spew venom at black conservatives would do well to read about the lives and philosophies of such luminaries as Booker T. Washington, George Washington Carver, Frederick Douglass, Harriet Tubman and many others who refused to subscribe to the victim mentality.

They should make an attempt to understand what it takes to ascend from the lifestyle of Southern sharecroppers to the office of secretary of state of the United States of America. Perhaps then they would rally to the side of Condoleezza Rice, who achieved this and much more including becoming a concert pianist. When the black community tolerates a group of liberal Rutgers professors who succeeded in disinviting Rice to their commencement because she is a black conservative, they embolden the controlling elites and dramatically minimize accomplishments that any ethnic group should be proud of.

We must fight for the precious hearts and souls of all of our young people. We have to give them the "can-do" attitude that characterized the rapid ascension of America. We must defang the dividers by ignoring them and thinking for ourselves.

I wish the haters and manipulators would take a moment to examine their hearts and motives. I hope they will think about using their intellectual talents for good. They would be wise to ask themselves this question: How much good did being one of the cool guys in high school do in the long run? Let us all give honor to the concepts of hard work, integrity, kindness, compassion, personal responsibility, family values, and faith in and obedience to God.

Many people from all backgrounds gave up their freedom, their blood and even their lives to provide a life of liberty and dignity for those trapped by the chains of legal discrimination and hatred. We must not allow their sacrifice to become meaningless by allowing "do-gooders" to substitute the chains of overt racism with the chains of dependency, low expectations, victimhood and misdirected anger.

~~~

Keeping Conservatives Focused on the Big Picture

April 9, 2014

Imagine a situation in which there is an earthquake that destroys a suspension bridge over a deep canyon.

A passenger train is speeding toward the location, and those in charge realize there is a potential problem ahead but choose instead to argue about the ambient temperature in the passenger cars, the food service and whether they will reach their final destination on time. A few people are quite disturbed when they learn of the tragedy about to unfold if the train isn't halted, but they are labeled as "alarmists" who really are not sophisticated enough to understand the situation.

Obviously, I am referring to our nation and the impending disaster that awaits us if we continue on a course of ever-expanding government control of our lives, fiscal irresponsibility, unwise energy policies and a laissez-faire attitude regarding our world leadership responsibilities.

Conservatives and other thinking individuals must recognize that we are in dire straits. They must adopt a sense of urgency in order to prevent irreparable damage to the concept of a nation where people are free to pursue their dreams without interference -- as long as they are not harming others.

They should not be arguing among themselves over petty differences and refusing to support individuals who largely agree with them about the direction of the country but perhaps have some disagreements about issues that easily could be resolved after the disaster has been averted.

It is troubling to see members of the tea party being attacked by establishment conservatives, and vice versa. If they get angry when their candidate loses in a primary race and refuse to support the winner, they are playing right into the hands of the progressives, from whom they could learn much.

Currently, there are two major visions for America. Liberals envision an overarching central government that controls all of the resources and ensures "equitable" redistribution in a way that prevents anyone from suffering hardship, regardless of their lifestyle and life choices.

The conservative vision emphasizes personal responsibility and a governmental role confined by the U.S. Constitution. This is the vision that was embraced by our founders.

The liberal vision, however, seems to be rapidly gaining momentum, even though many of its proponents would argue that either the government is not really trying to take control, or authority is a necessary function in its role of determining qualifications for licenses, setting standards and establishing such things as age requirements for public school attendance.

These big-government proponents also argue that Obamacare is no more intrusive on our freedoms than other forms of government regulation. This indicates a lack of understanding of the liberal nature of governmental control, which eventually results in authoritarian oversight of virtually every aspect of our lives. By encircling businesses, educational institutions and health care enterprises with massive regulatory shackles, the government eventually will be able to shut down virtually any entity that refuses to cooperate with its mandates.

For example, recently, the last lead-smelting plant in the United States was shut down by the Environmental Protection Agency for violating some of those regulatory shackles. That certainly could be seen as a victory for some who are interested in decreasing the amount of ammunition available to gun owners.

Putting the Internal Revenue Service in charge of the enforcement of the components of Obamacare establishes a situation where the most feared government agency is empowered to wreak havoc on the lives of citizens who express dissent. It is quite astonishing that many are unable to fathom this danger and thus dismiss it -- much like those in charge of the passenger train speeding toward danger.

Liberals have just as many disagreements among themselves as conservatives. Still, in order to accomplish their goals, they have learned to put aside their differences and create large, loyal voting blocs. Sometimes they make empty promises, but by repeating them often, people actually believe that they are benefiting, when, in fact, the opposite may be occurring.

Liberals appear to be quite comfortable with a health care bill that was passed with obvious deceit emanating from the highest levels of government. Very much like the radical Islamists who believe any means is acceptable to accomplish their goals, many in the liberal movement are willing to relegate to the sidelines the Judeo-Christian values that so rapidly elevated our country.

Conservatives shouldn't emulate this deception, but they ought to learn to present a united front to harness the power and energy necessary to reverse the downward spiral of the greatest nation in the history of the world.

We must look at the big picture and concentrate our efforts on establishing responsible fiscal policies, fair taxation, responsible energy and environmental policies, and empowerment through education. Many social issues can be dealt with in time, including entitlement reform. To worry about these issues before addressing the failing economy is a mistake.

The dismal state of the current economy, as indicated by the falling labor-force participation rate, is conducive to the further development of big-government programs. By the same token, the policies that will result in an explosion of the economy will make entitlement reform much easier.

If we focus on the big picture, everyone will win.

~~~

Recovering America's Exceptionalism

April 16, 2014

In 1831, Alexis de Tocqueville, the famous French historian, came to America to study our nation. Europeans and others were fascinated with the success of the fledgling nation, then barely 50 years old and already competing on the world stage.

Such a thing had never before occurred, and Tocqueville was determined to discover the secret. He was duly impressed by our governmental structure, including the separation of powers, but he was in awe of the public educational system, which rendered its recipients completely literate by the completion of second grade. This depth of education was generally only found among the aristocracy in Europe.

Let's put aside the diversionary arguments about lack of educational access for all, which was a huge mistake, and concentrate on the tremendous advantage afforded our predecessors by education. Early settlers not only mastered reading, writing and arithmetic, but also shared practical skills, all of which enabled them to traverse and tame a rugged and frequently hostile terrain from sea to shining sea.

As isolated communities sprang up throughout the nation, they were able to thrive through innovation, industry and compassion. The "can-do" attitude involved hard labor, but it also included a sense of responsibility for those who through injury or other hardships could no longer care for themselves. The spirit of caring, although diminished, remains an important part of who we are today.

Tocqueville was impressed by the fiery sermons that emphasized the word of God and not the social mores of the day. He concluded his American analysis by saying, "America is great because she is good. If America ever ceases to be good, she will cease to be great." America was different because we openly acknowledged the role of God in our lives.

Some will say, "Carson is a religious fanatic because he believes in God and the Bible." Interestingly, the very same people are quick to invoke the name of God and recommend prayer at times of national and personal tragedy. Hypocrisy is their frequent companion.

Some will say America can never make claims of "goodness" owing to her history of slavery. Although it was by far the worst atrocity in our history, we paid a horrendous price in lives lost or destroyed in a Civil War that all but incapacitated a young nation. The guilt, shame and humility that resulted from this dark American episode will teach us and stigmatize us well into the future. Learning from mistakes is a sign of wisdom and goodness.

What is disturbing in the pursuit of goodness is the turning of a blind eye toward corruption, much like the Romans did before the fall of their empire. Episodes such as the Internal Revenue Service scandal should alarm all Americans, regardless of political affiliation. The fact that one party has characterized it as a "phony scandal" tells you a great deal about the loss of honesty in our society.

The fact that one party is willing to use its majority status to cram a health care bill down the throats of the minority party and the American people and then refuses to acknowledge the obvious illegitimacy of a bill passed largely on the basis of false information provides a barometer on the lack of importance placed on virtue in our society today. How can such a society in any way claim to be good?

How can a society that kills millions of innocent unborn babies and then labels anyone opposing the practice "anti-woman" claim even a modicum of goodness? How can a nation that uses its news media to subtly trash traditional families, promote a drug-filled lifestyle and ridicule faith in God claim the mantle of righteousness?

I could go on pointing out how far we have strayed from our Judeo-Christian roots. For some, such a departure cannot come soon or dramatically enough. However, I believe the majority of Americans understand that we are different from everyone else, and that difference had a great deal to do with our rapid rise to the pinnacle of world power and wealth.

As we depart from our former values of decency, honesty, compassion and fairness, our status as a blessed nation will also be diminished.

Our decline is not necessary if we can learn from the mistakes of others and reclaim the values upon which our nation was built. I am not advocating for a national religion, but I do think we should seriously consider the words of John Adams, who said, "Our Constitution was made only for a moral and religious people. It is wholly inadequate for the government of any other."

America can be great, but it requires real courage and conviction to resist the urge to be "cool." None of this means we should impose Judeo-Christian values on those who wish to adopt a different kind of lifestyle, but it does mean we should not allow an alternative lifestyle to be imposed upon us.

Fairness is a two-way street, and so is tolerance. If the majority refuses to fight for its rights, while a vocal minority uses a compliant media to try to fundamentally change America, we will have only ourselves to blame.

~~~

When Government Looks More Like Foe than Friend

April 23, 2014

The Cliven Bundy case in Nevada provides many insights into the state of our nation with respect to the relationship between the people and the government.

The Bundys appear to be honorable American citizens without adequate legal counsel to help resolve a federal land issue about which they disagree with the Bureau of Land Management. Without question, they violated some of the innumerable laws and regulations that continue to entangle every aspect of American life.

Their violations certainly could have been handled through a multitude of less brutal means than those employed by our federal government, which through the mouthpiece of Sen. Harry Reid emphasizes how important it is for the government to enforce its laws.

It is quite interesting to see, though, that those same bureaucrats refuse to enforce some of our federal border-protection laws and other domestic policies with which they disagree. Perhaps Reid's time could be better spent explaining why it is acceptable for the federal government to pick and choose which laws it wishes to enforce.

The senator readily referred to the Bundys and their supporters as "domestic terrorists," but the current administration is reticent about applying the same term to Maj. Nidal Malik Hasan, who admitted slaughtering more than a dozen people in 2009 at Fort Hood in Texas. What does this tell us about our government and its perceptions and alignments?

The massive show of federal force in the Bundy case is frightening because it gives us a brief glimpse of the totalitarian regime that awaits a sleeping populace that does not take seriously its voting responsibilities and places in public office (and returns to public office) people who do not represent traditional American values.

The fact that the ranchers were well armed and willing to literally fight for their rights probably tempered the enthusiasm of the federal forces to engage in further aggression. It was clear from the body language and from some of the reported verbal responses of the government forces that they were not prepared to engage in lethal combat with fellow Americans.

Those Americans who are concerned about the possible future imposition of martial law after a financial collapse or some other event should take solace in knowing that many military and law enforcement personnel would likely refuse to obey commands inconsistent with freedom and American values. Such commands could emanate from any political party in the future, but it is likely that such a party would be one controlling an administration that selectively enforces laws and ignores or excuses corruption.

Another important lesson from this incident is the value of a well-armed citizenry. The Second Amendment was crafted by wise citizens who recognized how quickly an enemy invasion could occur and how our own government could be deceived into thinking it had the right to dominate the people.

Such domination is considerably more difficult when people have arms and can put up significant resistance. This is the reason that brutal dictators like Fidel Castro, Josef Stalin, Mao Zedong, Adolf Hitler and Idi Amin tried to disarm the populace before imposing governmental control. Such domination could occur in America in the not too distant future if we are not vigilant.

We must be reasonable and willing to engage in conversation about how to limit the availability of dangerous weapons to criminals and violent or insane people. In light of past worldwide atrocities committed by tyrants, though, to threaten the Second Amendment rights of ordinary American citizens is itself insanity. Those wishing to ban assault weapons fail to understand the original intent of the Second Amendment.

Just as insidious as the attempt to limit weapons and ammunition to law-abiding citizens is the incessant invasion of privacy by the government. Unless there is reasonable cause for suspicion as determined by a court of law, there is no need for the government to know all of the intimate details of our lives, including whom we talk to, where we spend our time and money, or which weapons we own, provided we're not purchasing tanks or fighter planes.

For our nation to once again be a thriving metropolis of freedom and innovation, the people and the government must peacefully coexist in an atmosphere of trust and mutual respect. This can occur only when laws are equally enforced and political favors are a thing of the past. When obvious governmental corruption is discovered, it must be swiftly and openly dealt with, and the perpetrators must face easily verifiable punishment.

This is just the opening salvo of what a trustworthy and honorable government should strive for. If we had such a government, border enforcement would be a given, the rights of the people would be respected, and events like the incident between the Bundys and the Bureau of Land Management would not occur.

We the people of the United States are the only ones capable of preventing uncontrolled government expansion and abuse. Like the ranchers in Nevada, Americans must find the courage and determination to maintain a free and vibrant nation. Government should be our friend and ally. When it is, we should support it wholeheartedly.

~~~

Cleaning Skeletons Out of the Closet

April 30, 2014

With Europeans intrigued by America's unexpected success, Alexis de Tocqueville carried out an in-depth study of the new nation in the 1830s. He was quite impressed with our divided government, which featured the separation of powers.

This structure made it difficult for any one branch -- executive, judicial or legislative -- to acquire too much power and run roughshod over the other branches and the will of the American people. Unfortunately, today we are witnessing a largely unchecked executive branch issuing decrees that circumvent Congress while facing only tepid resistance.

In civilian life, when a contract is entered into by two parties, and it is subsequently discovered that one side knowingly presented false promises in order to consummate the deal, a legitimate lawsuit can be initiated on the basis of fraud. The Affordable Care Act is a prime example of such a contract in the form of a bill, which never would have been passed if it had been revealed that millions of people would lose the health insurance with which they were satisfied and that they might not be able to keep their doctors, among other promises.

Nevertheless, this massive case of fraud has not been legally challenged by the legislative branch, leaving one to wonder why.

We hear a great deal about "Chicago-style politics." It is nothing more than a euphemism for political corruption, including bullying, blackmail and bribery. These pressures can be just as easily applied to national political figures as to local politicians.

Courage can be quite difficult to find when the threat of exposure hangs over one's head. In an age when Big Brother is capable of watching everything we do, it is not hard to imagine a scenario in which large numbers of public servants are silenced or subdued by secretive threats.

I have had an opportunity to witness firsthand how the blackmail threat operates. Several years ago, while I was in the operating room, I received a call from one of the legal offices at Johns Hopkins University informing me that the state of Florida was trying to attach my wages for child support.

I was shocked at such an allegation and informed them that I have three children, which I already support very ably. They said a woman in Florida was accusing me of being the father of her son, and that she had proof of our relationship. The proof turned out to be knowledge of where I went to high school, college and medical school, and where I served my internship and residency. To top all of that off, she had a picture of me in scrubs. I said anyone could obtain such information. However, the paternity suit was pursued, and I had to involve my personal lawyer.

As the case advanced, I was asked to provide a blood specimen to facilitate DNA testing. I refused on the basis of the incompetence of any governmental agency that was willing to pursue a paternity suit on such flimsy grounds. I said that level of incompetence would probably result in my blood specimen being found at a murder scene and my spending the rest of my life in prison.

Shortly thereafter, the suit was dropped with no further ramifications. I'm virtually certain that the woman in Florida erroneously assumed that someone who travels as much as I do was engaging in numerous extramarital affairs and wouldn't even remember all of the parties with whom they had been involved. Under such circumstances, she assumed I would be willing to fork over the money to avoid public embarrassment.

What she didn't know is that I did not have to scratch my head and try to remember which affair she represented, because I know that the only woman I have ever slept with in my life is my wife. Even if that had not been the case, I think confession and dealing with the consequences would have been the best course of action.

In the early history of America, Treasury Secretary Alexander Hamilton was seduced by the wife of a political enemy with the intention of blackmailing him into complying with their wishes. Hamilton publicly confessed his transgression, and the public forgave him, completely thwarting the plans of his adversaries.

I think the American people are just as forgiving today if people are willing to be honest. With so much at stake regarding our country's future, I think now would be an excellent time to come clean for all national public figures who have been threatened by Chicago-style politics or who know that there are skeletons in their closets.

If it were all done in a short time span, the media would be overwhelmed, and the people would quickly understand the extent of the disgusting and dishonest practices infesting the highest levels of government.

Importantly, our public officials would be able to act with courage and conviction to rectify the corrupt practices that are all too readily ignored and that threaten the moral fabric of our nation. I am confident that the American people would be both forgiving and grateful for the willingness of public figures to take a risk to preserve the American way of life.

~~~

Rethinking America's Decline

May 7, 2014

We recently learned that China is poised to replace the United States as the No. 1 economic power in the world sometime later this year. Our anemic quarterly growth rate of 0.1 percent certainly lends credence to this speculation. We must seriously question those who say our nation is not in decline. They are adopting the ostrich strategy and sticking their heads in the sand.

There is no question that America is the pinnacle nation of the world and is likely to remain in that position for several years, given our military strength and the depth and stability of our financial infrastructure. However, overconfidence is the frequent companion of catastrophic decline, as confirmed by numerous historical writings. If we continue our fiscally irresponsible ways, coupled with our arrogance, there exists no other possibility than self-ruination.

Our ability to print money is already in jeopardy, as other nations have been making noise about altering the international reserve-currency system to emphasize multiple currencies, elevating their status and decreasing the strength of the U.S. dollar. Our ever-increasing national debt would then place us on shaky ground. The Treasury securities we have been offering to China and others would no longer hold the same appeal, and all the borrowing we have done against the financial well-being of our progeny will come back to plague us and them.

Many who are responsible for putting us in this precarious position would argue that we don't need to worry about countries such as China replacing us, because they have too many structural problems. China is far behind us in per-capita income, creating many social issues and negatively impacting growth of the middle class, which is the most effective growth engine.

Their paucity of appropriate environmental controls has led to lethal industrial pollution, encouraging some of the intellectually gifted and mobile citizens to leave the country. China also has a weak banking system, with too much government interference, which means their currency is unlikely to be accepted by the rest of the world as the reserve currency for many years. They could, however, recognize and correct these deficiencies more rapidly than expected, thereby enhancing their position as a formidable challenger to the United States.

Even if these problems are rectified, China cannot expect continuation of its recent economic expansion, which is already dissipating. If the United States has the good sense to significantly lower its corporate-tax rate, this dissipation will accelerate. Additionally, the lack of intellectual private-property protection in China will prevent it from generating the kind of innovation that usually accompanies pinnacle-nation status.

When it comes to energy, China has large potential reserves of shale gas, but lacks natural water in those areas, making extraction difficult without new technology. We may be unable to exploit this weakness because of self-imposed, shortsighted overregulation of the energy sector in our country.

From these few examples, it can be seen that a combination of wise moves by China and unwise moves by the U.S. in the next few years could have very troubling implications for the future of our country.

If there is a sudden, cataclysmic debt-engendered U.S. financial crisis, China is only one of a number of possible successors to our position. Perhaps our energy should be spent figuring out how to avoid financial collapse and also invigorate the most powerful economic engine the world has ever known. We should take advantage of the great laboratory of ideas: successful states that have gone from severe budgetary deficits to significant surpluses through actions of wise governors and legislative bodies. Let's look at their taxation policies and the business conditions they created that stimulated economic activity. There is nothing partisan about this approach. It would be a manifestation of common sense, which should know no political affiliation.

The economic problems we are experiencing in this country fortunately are induced by our own ineptitude. I say fortunately, because it is within our power to alter our course. We do not have to depend on the good will of someone else. When we work together, as was the case with the Simpson-Bowles commission on fiscal responsibility, excellent ideas can be generated that could move us along the path of economic recovery. As was the case with the Roman Empire, our fate is in our hands.

~~~

Leaders Who Fail To Own Up To Mistakes Are Unfit for Office

May 14, 2014

The recent escalating arguments over whether there should be further congressional hearings on Benghazi are troubling. The fact that there are substantial numbers of people who feel that there is nothing more to investigate when four American lives were lost and no one has answered for this crime provides an indication of how far our sense of justice has slipped.

This should not be a partisan issue, because the implications of ignoring or prevaricating about the underlying mistakes will have far-reaching consequences. The United States has diplomatic establishments throughout the world, and if they can be attacked without consequences, it greatly diminishes our influence despite any protestations to the contrary.

What does it say about our judgment if we have diplomatic establishments for which we make inadequate provisions for protection? This is especially disturbing because it was revealed that requests by the consulate in Benghazi for more protection were refused. There had been attacks on the consulate not long before the fatal attack, and hostile actions had been taken against the British, which they were wise enough to react to appropriately.

Even more confounding was the decision to abandon our personnel at the consulate because someone decided that our military forces could not reach them in time to effect a rescue. How could such a decision be made when no one knew how long the hostile action would last? Several military personnel who were in the area ignored orders to stand down and instead rushed to the consulate with assault weapons and resisted hostile forces long enough to allow some of their colleagues to escape, while sacrificing their own lives. Their heroic actions demonstrate the bravery and loyalty that characterize American military forces. I feel certain that those men had no doubt in their minds that reinforcements were on the way, and that if they could just hold out long enough, their efforts would be rewarded.

When our top officials make decisions to abandon our own people because they feel the situation is hopeless, they also abandon the concept of American exceptionalism and create doubt in the minds of all future military participants about the intention of their superiors to expend maximum effort to preserve their lives when they have sacrificed everything for our nation.

Making mistakes is part of being human, but the ever-increasing deception that is necessary to cover those mistakes when honesty is abandoned is evil. Those willing to ignore evil for political reasons should question their fitness for leadership of our nation. In this case, a blatant falsehood was promoted -- namely that the Obama administration had international terrorist activity directed at America under control, and that the Benghazi incident was a spontaneous action resulting from the outrage of locals who had viewed an offensive anti-Islamic video. Undue importance was placed on promoting an image of U.S. strength during the weeks immediately preceding the presidential election of 2012.

Again, I must emphasize that if we, the American people, the American press and the American political class, participate in the cover-up or ignore such an important story, we contribute to the demise of honesty and truth as pillars of our governing structure. In the book of Proverbs, King Solomon put it this way: "If a ruler listens to lies, those who serve him will be wicked."

We also should be concerned about the attempt by some to ignore or downgrade the significance of the Internal Revenue Service (IRS) scandal. The fact that something this contrary to the concept of freedom can happen in a country based on constitutional values and be characterized as a "phony scandal" by people who supposedly have the best interests of this country at heart again points to the danger of placing partisan politics above truth and honesty.

When politicians huddle and try to figure out ways to defend their leader or their party and ignore the well-being of their nation, the people must take notice and do everything within their power to make sure they are represented by those who share their beliefs, and not by those who are simply party loyalists.

Obviously, the IRS was used in inappropriate ways, or Lois Lerner would not have pleaded the Fifth Amendment. It is more than disturbing that the president of the United States and many in his party feigned outrage when the inappropriate actions of the IRS initially were exposed, but now cannot lend support to a full and unfettered investigation of activities that threaten the very liberty of the American people.

A bipartisan group should investigate both Benghazi and the IRS scandal in a transparent manner. If wrongdoing is discovered, those responsible must face consequences, and procedures must be established to ensure that such abuses never occur again.

Most importantly, the people must awaken and look objectively at the actions of both Democrats and Republicans and not simply accept what party leaders say. Freedom is not free, and vigilance in responsible voting is necessary to preserve it.

~~~

Charting a Course Between Principle and Pragmatism

May 21, 2014

I recently was asked how I could possibly endorse the U.S. Senate candidacy of Dr. Monica Wehby, who is running as a Republican from Oregon. She is pro-choice, which in the opinion of many makes her unacceptable as a conservative.

I called her to query her about her stance on this issue. She stated that personally, she is very pro-life, but she feels the government has no business interfering with the relationship between the mother, the baby, the doctor and God. I feel differently, because if abolitionists had taken a similar hands-off approach, I might not have been free to write this column. As someone who has spent a lifetime trying to save the lives of children, even with intrauterine surgery, it is probably not difficult to imagine why I am extremely oriented toward efforts to preserve human life, especially innocent human life that has yet to experience the extrauterine world.

Given this pro-life propensity, one might ask how I could endorse someone who is pro-choice. The answer is this: I'm not an ideologue who determines a person's worthiness with a litmus test. I have known Wehby as a friend and colleague for many years, and she is extremely intelligent and knows how to make decisions based on evidence versus ideology. Also, in a state like Oregon, which is left-leaning, she would not be a viable candidate if she maintained a pro-life stance.

If conservatives are going to win in 2014 and 2016 and preserve the environment of freedom to which we have grown accustomed, it will be necessary to learn how to prioritize issues. I am not saying that social issues are not important, but if the executive branch remains in the hands of those with "secular progressive" ideas in 2016, and two or three more Supreme Court justices with similar leanings are appointed, conservative social ideas will become anathema to the prevailing powers, who will use every tool available to them to silence such opposition.

The extreme intolerance of the left for opinions that vary from their own has been amply demonstrated on university campuses, in the mainstream media and in the public square in recent years. Boycotting those with whom they disagree is insufficient for them, as demonstrated by their attempts to put their political adversaries out of business or assassinate their character.

Sometimes it is not possible to go from a position of extreme weakness to one of great power in one fell swoop. We must realize that getting people into office who agree with us 90 percent of the time is far superior to ending up with someone who opposes you at every opportunity at the behest of their party leaders. With patience and good leadership, the 90 percenters could be moved in the right direction and would be great allies in redirecting our country toward common-sense solutions for our multitude of problems.

The soul of America is at stake, and the future of our children and their children is threatened by unsustainable growing debt. Those who just listen to propaganda and refuse to read history or familiarize themselves with basic financial knowledge are easily fooled by those claiming that we are safe because our debt is rising more slowly. Those who go off the financial cliff die whether they fall one mile or 10 miles. The point is this: If the country is destroyed, many other issues become irrelevant. We need to stabilize the country first and then address the other serious problems.

Although several variations now exist on the best way to perform cardiopulmonary resuscitation (CPR), in the past there was much confusion. In the early 1960s, a mnemonic device called the ABCs of CPR was popularized and eliminated much of the confusion. The proper order of the procedure was easy to recall by remembering what each letter stood for. "A" was for "airway," which can be quickly optimized. "B" was for "breathing" to remind the rescuer of the importance of oxygenation, and "C" was for "circulation," which could be re-established by chest compression. For example, if chest compression is started in someone with an obstructed airway, it might prove less effective. By prioritizing the steps, many lives were saved.

If a ship is about to suffer massive destruction by sailing over Niagara Falls, why devote energy to scraping the barnacles off the bottom? There will be plenty of time for that once the ship is saved. Worrying about the barnacles before reversing course detracts from critical action. Enough said.

This rationale will anger some who feel that their important issue, be it homosexual marriage, abortion, illegal immigration or Second Amendment rights, should never be anywhere except front and center. I sympathize with those sentiments, but as a pragmatist, I realize that if conservatives continue to be fragmented over issues on which there will never be unanimous agreement, they will never get the chance to address these issues down the road. Principles are important -- but so are wisdom and savvy when building consensus with people with different principles.

~~~

Conservatives Won't Win Elections by Refusing To Compromise

May 28, 2014

More discussion on the topic of pragmatism and politics is critical. If conservatives decide to take their marbles and go home rather than fight to the bitter end because they feel their principles have been compromised, they will needlessly subject future generations to untold misery.

Voting for someone who agrees with you 90 percent of the time is far superior to voting for someone who disagrees with you 100 percent of the time. This is exactly what will happen if people refuse to exercise their civic duty and boycott elections because they feel betrayed. Personally, I am not supportive of abortion at all, but I can support people who feel differently if, in the gigantic scheme of things, they can help put an end to the murder of innocent babies. This is especially true of those who are personally inclined to save and protect life.

Perhaps an illustration is in order: Two armies are engaged in a war. Let's call the good army that is trying to defend an entire society the red army and the bad army that is trying to invade and pillage society the blue army. The blue army occupies a superior strategic position and is composed of slightly more troops, putting the red army at a distinct disadvantage. Some in the red army feel that they are right and, therefore, should simply march directly into battle with the blue army because right always wins.

Fortunately, some members of the red army are wise and have a better plan. They send a battalion of troops to the base of the mountain occupied by the blue army to distract them while the vast majority of red troops approach the mountain from the backside. They descend upon the blue army by surprise, completely vanquishing them and winning the war. The decoy red battalion may have sustained some casualties, but in the long run, the war was won, and the entire society was saved.

I hope this illustration is useful in helping some to understand that achieving a critical mass of conservatives and RINOs (Republicans in Name Only, as some call them) in office will ensure that we can get non-activist Supreme Court and federal judges in place who respect the U.S. Constitution. It is essential to achieve a critical mass of individuals in the U.S. House and Senate who can join with a president in upholding the Constitution. These representatives must believe in personal responsibility and creating a business-friendly environment, understand the balance between abundant fossil-fuel development and environmental safety, and yearn to elevate the government-dependent 47 percent rather than make them more dependent. They also must be totally pro-life and believe that the rule of law can undo a host of damaging regulations and restore the value system that made this nation great.

In the long run, with the help of God, we will be in a position to save millions of babies who otherwise would be slaughtered. With this kind of responsible empowerment, energizing a sluggish economy, bringing stability to a leaderless planet and facilitating innovation will not be that difficult. To sit helplessly by and pray for deliverance when the tools to achieve victory are in our hands is not useful. God helps those who help themselves.

Conservatives and those who share their values are the last bastion between freedom and tyranny. If the secular liberals, who are very clever, succeed in dividing us during the next two national elections, America as we know it will be gone. We can stop this, but we must work together. I disagree with those who think it is going to take decades to undo the damage that already has been done. Americans are exceptional and extremely resilient. We cannot allow ourselves to be defined by those who wish to fundamentally change our society.

I am convinced that Americans with common sense will soon regain power. It is essential that we not use the opportunity to exact revenge upon the liberals. Rather, we must govern by the Constitution in a way that is fair for all. It is not reasonable to have favorites and to enforce laws selectively. Most importantly, it is not the place of our government to rule the people; the government must always remember that it is in place to serve the people.

I believe that when people who were being manipulated by the secular liberals, including the media, have an opportunity to see how much better off they are when the proper relationship between the people and the government is restored, they will adopt a different attitude. This will empower them and the entire nation.

Now is the time to rise above partisan politics and recognize the incredible blessings God has bestowed upon our nation. It is time to elevate common sense, decency, honesty and compassion to their proper positions. Rather than simply repeating the words, we must actually achieve "one nation under God, indivisible, with liberty and justice for all."

~~~

One Nation Is Still Possible

June 4, 2014

My wife and I currently are on a book tour by bus through several states, and I have been struck by the number of people who already have read "One Nation," but also by the large, enthusiastic crowds whose constituents include all political parties. People are concerned about our future as a nation and the poor prioritization of issues by our leaders, to put it mildly.

We wrote "One Nation" to convince our fellow Americans that "we the people" are not enemies and that our strength is derived from unity and common sense, which should be ubiquitous. The real enemies are the forces that are constantly trying to divide and conquer. They create divisions based on race, gender, age, education and, especially, income. It is important that we discuss who the purveyors of division are and what drives them to seek a radical alteration of the American way of life.

We discuss the tools used to manipulate the populace into feeling that they should be offended so easily by words, while diverting their attention away from the real issues that desperately cry out for a solution. One of the major keys to avoiding manipulation is knowledge. Our system of government was designed for people who could easily understand the issues and vote intelligently based on knowledge, rather than blindly following political leaders who are often enshrouded with less than honorable motives.

One of the book's major themes is that knowledge is a formidable enemy of falsehood and a formidable ally of truth. There are specific steps that each of us can take, such as reading about something new for a half-hour every day for a year. Such a simple move will profoundly change the life of the reader and will vastly increase their effectiveness as an involved and responsible citizen.

In today's world of widely disseminated information, a person rapidly can become knowledgeable in a variety of areas, regardless of his occupation.

The greatest concerns of the people we are encountering on the road revolve around the future of their children and grandchildren as we continue along the path of government growth and escalating expenditure of taxpayer money, essentially ensuring that future generations have lives characterized by significantly reduced economic freedom.

The lessons are abundant in America and throughout the world regarding the consequences of prolonged fiscal irresponsibility. Also, historical records are replete with accounts of the self-destruction of nations, driven by national debt. Many of our leaders are complacent about our precarious financial state because people seem more interested in reality television and sporting events than in our imminent financial collapse. Once again, history informs us that national leaders seldom recognize and act upon economic warnings before disaster occurs.

I think the majority of the American people know we are rapidly approaching the fiscal cliff, and they are concerned but not panicked. It is not too late for people of all political stripes to put partisan bickering aside and join forces to combat the unsustainable debt that threatens our future. It also is not too late for responsible voters to notice which leaders refuse to seriously engage in such endeavors and remove them from office.

It doesn't matter to me that those who despise my warnings will say I'm only promoting my book and trying to make money. From their perspective, they are probably incapable of understanding motives that would differ from theirs. Regardless of what they say, November 2014 will bring perhaps the most consequential midterm elections in history. Combined with the elections of 2016, "we the people" will determine whether traditional American values and traditional interpretations of our Constitution are important to us, or whether we prefer to continue down the path of ever-increasing government control of everything, including our lives. Books such as "One Nation: What We Can All Do To Save America's Future" will, by the grace of God, ensure that we go into that election process with our eyes open.

Not only are there no enemies among us, but we can and must come together to recapture the values that made us an exceptional nation. We must use our intellect and energy to unleash the most powerful economic engine the world has ever known. Then we must concentrate on opening the pathways of personal empowerment to the millions of Americans who feel forgotten. Instead of restraining them in positions of dependency, we must provide clear pathways to self-improvement. We can help those who have made mistakes that make it difficult for them to pursue an education by providing a reasonable amount of money for day care.

By demonstrating true compassion as dictated by Judeo-Christian values, we can make America a place of dreams and success for everyone. We must remember that freedom is not free, and all of us must be involved in its maintenance.

~~~

Liberal Denizens of the Fourth Estate Present a Distorted View of America

June 11, 2014

There is no question that a free, honest and unbiased press is a great asset to any free and fair society. A press characterized by integrity demands answers to hard questions from everyone, regardless of political affiliation. When the media choose sides, it enables those on the selected side to ignore rules and conduct themselves as they please, having no one to whom they must answer. Of course, this assumes the populace is largely asleep at the wheel and not demanding objectivity of the press.

Unfortunately, the "mainstream media" and the American people have conformed to this latter description in recent years, but I see signs of the people beginning to recognize the risks to both political and economic freedom imposed by the continuation of a journey down that pathway. Like politicians, the media no longer enjoy the almost unanimous trust they once could take for granted. What has caused so much of the media to become biased and agenda-driven, and why has the partiality become so blatant?

I think the answer revolves around the fact that we as a nation are at a critical decision point. We are one or two national elections away from determining whether we want to continue down the road toward "utopia," where all of our basic needs are met from cradle to grave, the only price being total subservience to the government, or alternatively, to reverse direction and go back up the road toward personal responsibility and embrace the "can-do" attitude and values that facilitated the rapid rise of America on the world stage.

The proponents of each of these lifestyles are convinced that they are right, and it will be difficult to convince them otherwise. Because many so-called "progressives" reject the traditional American way of life and wish to fundamentally change us, I think they have an obligation to fully engage in the debate about why their vision is better. Many of these liberals dwell in the mainstream media and seem reluctant to engage in serious conversation. Instead, they attempt to ask leading questions of their opponents and then distort the answers in an attempt to diminish their "enemy" in the eyes of the public. If they are successful, they never have to actually address the real issue for which they have no real answers.

It is encouraging that many people are seeing the light and ignoring the intellectually bankrupt assertions of these agents of resentment. We should teach our children and everyone in our spheres of influence to recognize these disgusting and dishonest techniques and reject them. As was the case on the third-grade playground in elementary school, it is best to ignore the name-callers and proceed with more important endeavors.

Over the past year, I have learned a great deal about the press in America. It is not uniformly unfair with nefarious agendas, but a significant portion is. One of the best ways to determine which news organizations are objective and which have an agenda is to keep a scorecard that lists both electronic and print media. When evaluating a story, check off whether it is concentrating on factual reporting or demonization. If there is controversy, determine whether both points of view are considered. If major stories of a political nature are ignored or barely mentioned, that should raise suspicions about objectivity.

My emergence on the national political scene has produced great consternation for many in the media who adhere to the "progressive" ideology. The fact that I had a difficult upbringing and embraced the concept of personal responsibility and hard work, rather than dependency, directly opposes their narrative that people must depend on public support and remain loyal to the party that provides for their maintenance. In fairness to many of the liberals, because of that background and my storybook-like career in medicine, they considered me a brilliant role model and hero until it became clear that I reject the liberal model of "success." At that point, they deemed me a pariah who could no longer think for himself, an obvious tool of conservatives. If they stopped for a minute and thought about how silly that sounds, they might once again be able to find some noble bearings.

Many have said to me that the mainstream media are hopelessly biased and cannot be reformed. I included an analysis of them in my latest book, "One Nation," which is too extensive for this column, but the bottom line is this: No one is hopeless. We should continue to try to engage all media in conversations about important issues, while rejecting their attempts at demonization and divergence.

I think it is still possible for jaded members of the press to realize that they have a higher calling than blind and misguided loyalty to their chosen heroes, even at the risk of national destruction. Objective journalistic integrity can play a tremendous role in healing an ailing nation. The issues we face as a nation deserve the attention of rational, mature and objective individuals who have the courage to seek the truth, wherever it leads.

~~~

As Long as U.S. Leaders Game the System, So Will Illegals

June 18, 2014

In 2012, the current administration made it clear that certain unaccompanied illegal minors would not be deported if caught. This helped create an atmosphere of tolerance that would be conducive to the current rash of illegal dumping of thousands of children from south of the border into the United States. Now we have a humanitarian crisis that appears to have been manufactured for political reasons.

One would not have to be incredibly bright to predict that families in South and Central America, as well as in Mexico, would recognize a veiled invitation to get their children into the United States with little chance of deportation. Of course, the media are asking opponents of the administration for solutions to this crisis. Almost anything these opponents suggest will be either harsh, making them appear cruel and callous, or weak, making them appear to be amnesty supporters. Either way, they will take a political hit.

Meanwhile, the administration can stay above the fray and receive the political benefit of gratitude from many legal and illegal immigrants. It's a clever and effective ploy with the added benefit of redistributing even more American wealth. It remains to be seen how many people will be hoodwinked.

We all have heard it said many times that America is a land of immigrants, some voluntary and some involuntary. We have plenty of space in our country, but insufficient jobs and insufficient resources to support everyone who wants to come here. When we see innocent children used as political pawns, it still tugs at our heartstrings, which is the intent. The real question is: What are we going to do about it?

The combination of immigration reform being a tough issue and a political football has led to governmental stalemates and no useful solutions for decades. To begin to solve this problem, we must have some understanding of why it exists.

Despite all of its problems, America is still the place of dreams. As such, it is small wonder that so many from other nations would like to live here. The benefits of an American domicile are so great that they currently outweigh issues of legality.

Immigrating is relatively easy for those in proximity to the United States -- we have porous borders, and it is easy for illegals to hide and obtain fraudulent identification after they have penetrated the border. Although there is some fear of deportation, unenthusiastic and inconsistent enforcement of immigration laws is the expectation. Further incentives for illegal immigration are easy enrollment in public schools, easy employment for those willing to take jobs others don't want, easy access to health care and easy acquisition of public support through welfare programs. These and other inducements produce an osmotic effect that attracts ever more people to our land.

Any discussion of immigration reform should include bipartisan solutions to these inducements. If these issues are not addressed, solutions will fall short. On the other hand, if all of these issues are addressed firmly and consistently, the osmotic effect will be reversed. Just as people found a way to get here, they would find a way to leave on their own, and others would be less tempted to attempt illegal entry.

Detractors will say that if it were that simple, it already would have been done and we wouldn't be having this discussion. What they fail to account for is the fact that the issues have not been addressed.

A national guest-worker program makes sense and seems to work well in Canada. Noncitizens would have to apply for a guest-worker permit and have a guaranteed job awaiting them. Taxes would be paid at a rate commensurate with other U.S. workers, and special visas would allow for easy entry and egress across borders. Guest-worker status would be granted to individuals and not to groups.

People already here illegally could apply for guest-worker status from outside of the country, meaning they would have to leave first. They should in no way be rewarded for having broken our laws, but if they are wise, they would arrange with their employer before they leave to immediately offer them a legal job as soon as their application is received. When they return, they still would not be U.S. citizens, but they would be legal, and they would be paying taxes. Only jobs that are vacant as a result of a lack of interest by American citizens should be eligible for the guest-worker program.

It is essential that employers bear some responsibility for making sure that no illegal immigrants are hired. Employers who break the rules should receive swift, severe and consistent punishment that constitutes a real deterrent and not a mere inconvenience. A second infraction should be a criminal offense and treated as such.

All of this is irrelevant unless we have secure borders. There is much that can be learned from security personnel in prisons and other secured facilities, and there is a great deal of smart technology that could be employed to achieve secure borders. It is a matter of will rather than ability.

As long as we reward people who break laws, they will continue to break laws. We do need a continual flow of immigrants, but choosers need not be beggars. We make decisions based on our needs. People who refuse to comply with the rules must forfeit chances of legalization in the future. Anyone caught involved in voter fraud should be immediately deported and have his citizenship revoked.

The point is this: We must create a system that disincentivizes illegal immigration and upholds the rule of law while providing us with a steady stream of immigrants from other nations who will strengthen our society. Let's solve the problem and stop playing political football.

~~~

Playing a Name Game with the Redskins

June 25, 2014

The audacity of the U.S. Patent and Trademark Office in canceling the trademark of the Washington Redskins is frightening. When the government is in charge of deciding what is offensive and what is not, and has the power to punish the "offenders," we move further away from a free society and closer to a tyrannical nanny state.

We are not talking about a political issue that should have Democrats and Republicans coming down on different sides, but rather the fundamental freedom to express oneself, which is a part of the fabric of America. In the case of Dan Snyder, who owns the Redskins, he is being demonized for standing up for basic American principles. The team bore the same name when he purchased it in good faith. There was no indication at the time that subsequent demands for a name change would emerge, costing him millions of dollars in related expenses, not to mention lawsuits he might encounter by other businesses that could be injured by such a move.

There is no indication that many in the Native American community are upset after decades of the team's prominent and proud display of its mascot and name. This appears to be yet another case of purposefully induced hypersensitivity, providing yet another opportunity for unnecessary heavy-handed government tactics to infringe upon the peaceful existence of Americans.

I have had the pleasure of meeting Snyder, who is far from the demonic characterization seen in the gullible press, which allows itself to be manipulated by those wishing to bring about fundamental change in America. I do not doubt for one minute that the Redskins organization would change the name tomorrow if it thought it was truly offensive to most Native Americans.

Also, the majority of American citizens are still decent people who would not only demand a name change, but would vote with their feet and purses in a way that would send a loud and convincing message -- if they thought the name was offensive.

It appears that many have forgotten the power of free-market economic forces and instead have placed their trust in flawed government forces. Historically, individual freedoms vanish as government interventions increase.

Traditionally, sports teams choose mascots and names that bring them pride, rather than shame. There are numerous sports teams throughout the nation with colorful names and symbols, and they are not out to offend anyone. In a large, diverse society, it is likely that almost anything is offensive to someone. I suspect there are those who are offended by the fact that the Duke University basketball team is called the Blue Devils. Some would ridiculously opine that this nomenclature pays homage to the forces of evil. Should we cater to such foolishness, or should we grow up and focus on real issues, such as unacceptable rates of unemployment, terrorism, energy development, education, poverty, a stagnant economy, massive corruption, illegal immigration, growing national debt and many other things of greater importance?

We, the American people, must cease being distracted by peripheral issues and demand that our government officials focus their attention on the myriad problems that threaten to destroy our way of life. Like the ancient Romans, we are in danger of being distracted by relatively unimportant issues while our society crumbles beneath us. I challenge those who say I am exaggerating to a debate on this issue.

Many people equate political correctness with kind and compassionate speech. The two things are vastly different with very different purposes. Political correctness is meant to control thought patterns and speech content, creating unanimity and societal conformity, while kind and compassionate speech is meant to take into consideration the feelings and circumstances of others without compromising the truth. It is a much better alternative.

We need to be wary of those who attempt to convince groups of people that they should be offended by a word, phrase or symbol instead of concentrating on the real message being conveyed. These people remind me of the troublemakers in grade school who enjoyed watching the fallout from their devious ploys.

In today's politically correct society, we are in danger of extinguishing interpersonal communications altogether for fear of offending someone. All of this would be comically absurd if it were not so tragic and such an immense departure from the vision of a free and prosperous society that was envisioned by our Founders.

Rather than concentrating on unanimity of thought and speech, we must concentrate on extracting the meaning of verbal communications. Examining every word or phrase for possible offense is beyond stupid. More importantly, it is divisive and destructive. We must outright reject those who try to manipulate emotions for their own political advantage. The Founders of our nation were concerned about what would happen if the populace became uninformed and refused to think for themselves. They feared the day when Americans could be easily led and manipulated, which would lead to a drastic alteration of our nation.

The power to stop the erosion of our values and to restore common sense and prosperity to our nation is in our own hands. We must shake off the passivity and vigilantly guard against manipulation.

~~~

The Wisdom of Divided Government

July 2, 2014

House Speaker John Boehner recently shocked many of us when he announced that he is planning a lawsuit against the president for abuse of power. Many Americans feel that a harmonious working relationship between the branches of government has been seriously compromised in recent years. But when Alexis de Tocqueville visited America in 1831 to perform an in-depth analysis of the American phenomenon, he was impressed with our well-structured divided government and its separation of powers.

The writings of the founders of this nation certainly referenced the Bible frequently, but they also paid homage to the writings of Charles de Secondat, Baron de Montesquieu, who wrote prolifically about political theories. One of his most well-known works is "The Spirit of the Laws." In this book, he eloquently argues for the concept of separation of powers.

That argument seems to emanate from the Bible's book of Isaiah, 33:22, which states, "The Lord is our judge (judicial branch), the Lord is our lawgiver (legislative branch), the Lord is our King (executive branch)." Certainly this system of government has worked well for us in the past, helping to establish the United States of America as the most powerful nation the world has ever known within a relatively short period of time.

In order for a divided government to work, each branch must respect the other two branches. There always have been and always will be squabbles between the branches, but the big problem now is that the executive branch has decided to ignore anyone with whom it disagrees, including Congress.

Nowhere was this blatant disregard of Congress more clearly manifested than in President Obama's inappropriate "recess" appointments of three people to the National Labor Relations Board. He redefined the word "recess" in order to appoint individuals who might have a difficult time obtaining congressional approval.

This administration seems to have a penchant for redefining words to make them conform to its ideology. Obviously, if an individual can redefine anything anytime he wants to, he can manipulate virtually any situation into a favorable position for himself. If he is clever and no one notices, he can fundamentally change the foundational fabric of a society.

Passing a law in the usual legitimate fashion and then unilaterally changing that law is another thing this administration seems to cherish. Obamacare is a prime example of this tactic. For example, it would be like a ruler and his council passing a law against the growing of Brussels sprouts, much to the pleasure of his constituents. He then discovers that his favorite brother, who lives in Province A, is the largest farmer of Brussels sprouts in the region and is also his biggest financial supporter. He then unilaterally amends the law to exclude Province A, much to the displeasure of the populace, about whom he cares nothing. The point is that it is inconsistent with fairness to establish rules and then change them in the middle of the game without the consent of the other participants.

This article and many others could be spent detailing all of the instances that support the argument for executive branch overreach, but the truly important thing is to begin asking ourselves how we can reestablish a truly cooperative and harmonious balance of power aimed not at the enhancement of one political party or the other, but rather at providing life, liberty and the pursuit of happiness for the people. This is clearly what the people want, as indicated by their voting to put a liberal president in the White House and a conservative majority in the House of Representatives. The people of this country are not comfortable with runaway government in either direction.

Some will say that previous presidents issued even more executive orders than Obama. In some cases, this is true, but it is not the number of executive orders that is important. Rather, it is the effect of those orders, how they impact society and what precedents they set. When something is clearly wrong, citing a previous misdeed by someone else does not serve as adequate justification. This is like the kid who gets in trouble for hitting someone and says, "He hit me first." Because there is so much childish behavior in Washington, perhaps government officials need the same explanation as the children who fight: No one should be hitting anyone, and we should divert that energy to understanding the nature of the conflict and resolving it.

Civil conversations obviously would go a long way toward helping us as a nation to solve our problems. However, as Saul Alinsky said, "Never have a conversation with your adversary, because that humanizes him, and your job is to demonize him." This is why we see so much name-calling and finger-pointing these days, which is antithetical to our success as a nation.

When the pendulum swings once again to the right, it is vitally important that people with common sense govern according to the Constitution and in a way that respects the separation of powers. There can be no picking and choosing of laws to enforce, and no favoritism. The only special-interest group that should be considered is the American people.

~~~

Better Than Obamacare: Health Savings Accounts Would Be Free From Government Control

July 9, 2014

It's fortunate the Supreme Court of the United States saw it fit last week to rule that corporations could not be coerced into covering religiously objectionable forms of birth control for their employees.

This was a critical ruling, because it indicates that the majority of the Court still thinks religious beliefs and personal choice have a valid place in American society. The margin of the split decision, however, is alarming, because it reminds us of how close we are to having a government that will subject moral convictions to its bureaucratically directed control.

People have legitimate differences of opinion about the appropriateness of various forms of birth control, which is something most reasonable people on both sides of the political ledger understand. However, legally requiring the side opposed to a form of birth control to be financially responsible for its distribution to any employee who wants it is distinctly un-American and abusive to the concept of freedom of religion.

A major problem is that many people in our entitlement society see nothing wrong with forcing others to provide for their desires. In a free and open society, anyone should be able to purchase anything he or she wants that is legal. It really should be no one else's business. Common sense dictates, however, that it immediately becomes my business if I'm being forced to pay for it.

Wouldn't it be fairer and make more sense for people wanting some form of birth control to pay for it themselves? This is exactly what would happen if everyone had access to his or her own health savings account. A woman and her health care provider would decide on a birth control method, and the cost would be deducted from her account with no involvement of anyone else in any way. It's so simple and upholds privacy and freedom.

Health savings accounts can be funded in a variety of different ways and give people total control of where, how and with whom they wish to spend their health care dollars. Most people will want to get the biggest bang for the buck and will independently seek out both value and quality. That, in turn, will bring all aspects of medicine into the free-market economic model, thus automatically having an ameliorating effect on pricing transparency and quality of outcomes.

Many corporations and communities already have very positive experiences with health savings accounts. Those experiences could be further enhanced by allowing family members to shift the money in their accounts among themselves. For instance, if a family member was $500 short for a procedure or test, another family member could provide the money by authorizing its deduction from his account. This provides a whole other level of flexibility to the concept of health savings. The overwhelming majority of encounters with the medical world could be handled through this type of system, eliminating bureaucratic delays and frustration.

Under the multitudinous rules of Obamacare, the amount of money allowed to be managed through health savings accounts is severely restricted. Perhaps that is because the crafters of this gigantic, bureaucratic monstrosity realized that a well-functioning savings system would be easy to understand, much less expensive and give people control of their own health care. It would also eliminate two-tiered systems of health care, making every patient equally desirable from a business perspective. There should be no limit to the amount of money that can be contributed to and managed in an account. Money unspent at the end of the year should simply continue to accumulate without penalty.

If accounts are established at the time of birth, they will be even more potent, because the vast majority of people will not experience catastrophic or major medical events until well into adulthood. By that time, a great deal of money will have accumulated. Since bridge or catastrophic insurance will not be drawn upon for routine medical expenses, its costs will plummet, very much like homeowners insurance, which costs vastly less when there is a high deductible.

Somehow over the past few decades, we as a society have wandered away from the concept of using health insurance only for major medical issues and paying for routine services ourselves. This is largely responsible for the tremendous spike in medical costs. By using the health savings account system, we can return to a semblance of rational thinking.

The 5 percent of patients with complex pre-existing or acquired maladies would need to be taken care of through a different system, similar to Medicare and Medicaid but informed by the many mistakes in those programs from which we can learn. Even this kind of system should have elements of personal responsibility woven into it.

The bottom line: Health care for all of our citizens is the responsibility of a compassionate society and is well within our grasp, if we don't make it into a political football. The majority of Americans are unhappy with Obamacare and would prefer something that is simple, effective and under their own control. We do not have to settle for something imposed upon us for reasons other than good health care.

~~~

Cultivating a Curious Mind

July 16, 2014

I recently returned home after two weeks of engagements in New Zealand and Australia focusing on empowerment through reading. The Kiwis and Aussies are not very different from Americans, even though they inhabit the opposite side of the globe.

I was struck by the way many people perceived the political atmosphere in the United States. Although the well-educated individuals who have access to all of the American cable channels tend to be well informed on the issues, most people had only heard that America has finally repaired its broken medical system with the advent of Obamacare and now everyone, including the indigent, has excellent health care. They were under the impression that most Americans are very happy with Obamacare and with their wonderful president, who had ushered in a great new day in America with his brilliance in many areas.

Many people were shocked when I relayed the facts about the deleterious effects of Obamacare on employment, skyrocketing insurance premiums and the displacement of health care providers. Furthermore, they had little knowledge about Benghazi, the Internal Revenue Service scandal, the Veterans Affairs debacle or the depth of our financial woes. In other words, they were just like a multitude of Americans who pay little attention to their news sources and are not curious enough to seek multiple sources and arm themselves with enough historical knowledge to be able to decipher truth from fiction.

Fortunately, I found that most of the people Down Under are not nearly as dogmatic in their beliefs as Americans have become. Our people on either side of the political spectrum tend to be more close-minded, partaking only of news sources that align with their ideological beliefs and in many cases engaging in the demonization of other information sources. This, of course, leads to intolerance and ignorance, which are associated with a whole cadre of societal problems. Frequently, that narrow-mindedness is encouraged by hyper-partisan individuals who actually call out news outlets such as the Fox News Channel for ridicule.

Such people might do well to ask themselves what would become of our country if people only heard what the government wanted them to hear. If they could be honest with themselves, I think they would have to admit that they would be uncomfortable in that setting. The mainstream media could provide a great service to the American people, as well as people around the world, by embracing their duty to be objective investigators and reporters of the news. I realize the likelihood of that occurring is small, but hope springs eternal.

I was delighted with the enthusiasm for reading Down Under, and with the understanding that virtually any young person, regardless of their economic background, can empower himself with the knowledge that comes from reading. This acquisition of knowledge is the antidote to the herd mentality induced by an agenda-driven media.

Reading was emphasized so strongly among the early settlers of America that anyone who finished the second or third grade was completely literate, as is borne out in the beautiful prose that characterized the writing style and letters of the Western frontiers of America in the early 19th century. Many Southern aristocrats also exhibited impressive writing skills and understanding of the English language.

Interestingly, the same highly educated rulers forbade under enormous penalty the teaching of slaves to read. They fully understood how empowering education and knowledge are. It is likely that Frederick Douglass fled the plantation to escape the wrath of his master, who was displeased that his slave was learning to read. Slaves were supposed to be obedient and grateful for the magnanimous protection and provisions afforded them by their "wonderful" masters.

Today many people in America slavishly devote themselves to a political party without engaging in critical analysis of whether the philosophies of that party are really in sync with their true values and with the betterment of their position in society. If decades of such devotion leads to more broken families, more out-of-wedlock births, more involvement with the criminal justice system, more poverty and more dependency on government, maybe it is time to ask whether such devotion is warranted.

I was honored to be able to encourage many of the disadvantaged young people of Australia and New Zealand to take control of their own destinies through education and reading. I was thrilled by the trip sponsors' generous financial contributions to the Carson Scholars Fund, enabling us to reach more American students and emphasize the acquisition of knowledge and the development of humanitarian qualities.

I am convinced that the dream of our Founding Fathers of a free nation filled with knowledgeable and caring people who trust in God and accept personal responsibility is still possible. Each of us has a role to play in the realization of that dream. A big part of that role is self-education. We need to read all kinds of books and articles and experience a variety of electronic media. We should not engage in self-censorship, which creates a proclivity for indoctrination. I am convinced that a well-informed American populace will not be manipulated into relinquishing a beautiful American dream for all.

~~~

The Perils of Mixing Politics and Business

July 23, 2014

When I was a small child, one of the most dramatic and effective business boycotts in the history of America occurred. This, of course, was the Montgomery bus boycott. By refusing to ride the bus, blacks who were being discriminated against were able to terminate many discriminatory practices not only in Alabama, but throughout the South. The white-owned businesses were clearly being unfair, and the public transportation system was no better. The actions taken were appropriate and in many cases heroic.

The power of the purse, particularly in a capitalistic society, is mighty, and business boycotts are a potent tool in the hands of the masses to enforce economic and social fairness. Through the use of the ballot and the wallet, we the people have life-or-death power over virtually every aspect of our nation.

Astute business people generally do not make their political views widely known, because they realize that about half of their customers agree with them and half do not. There is no need to unnecessarily create animosity, especially when you are trying to sell products. In the case of Costco, a company highly respected for wise business practices, Jim Sinegal, the co-founder and former CEO, has made no secret of his profound admiration for President Obama and his policies.

For the sake of disclosure, I should reveal that I have been a member of the Costco board of directors for 15 years. There are people on the board of several political persuasions, and we are all friendly and work well together because politics plays no role in business decisions. In the years that I have had the privilege of serving on the board, I have never witnessed a single incident where politics influenced a business decision. Not only would that be unwise, but it would lead to mass resignations and membership cancellations, including yours truly.

Because of Sinegal's public support of Obama, the recent withdrawal of Dinesh D'Souza's book "America: Imagine a World Without Her" from Costco warehouses nationwide, just before the release of the movie by the same title, was widely interpreted as a political move -- the movie is very critical of the president. I spoke to current Costco CEO Craig Jelinek, who was so absorbed in the business of the company that he had been unaware of the movie prior to the resultant backlash. He readily admitted that those responsible for managing the limited book space in Costco warehouses should have been aware of the imminent release of the movie and retained the book in anticipation of a brisk stimulation of book sales, which had been sluggish.

Costco, once everybody's favorite place, suffered a major black eye, not because of an inappropriate injection of politics into the business world, but rather owing to an uncharacteristic lack of attention to what was going on in a small segment of the sales portfolio.

Through my budget-management experiences as a division director at Johns Hopkins for many years, and through many tough financial experiences as the president and co-founder of the Carson Scholars Fund, which is active in all 50 states, I gained enormous knowledge of business practices, but that pales in significance to what I have learned as a board member of both Costco and the Kellogg Co. during the past 17 years.

Managing and growing large multinational corporations requires wisdom and experience, and I have enjoyed the opportunity to work with and learn from both politically liberal and conservative business executives. I can honestly say that wise business practices transcend political ideology, and those who intentionally inject their politics into their business do so at their own peril. Their actions will be interpreted, rightly or wrongly, based on their political views.

In the case of Costco and the D'Souza book, lack of awareness was interpreted by many conservative customers as political misconduct because of Sinegal's views. Although he and I differ politically, he continues to be a huge financial supporter of the Carson Scholars Fund and many other educational endeavors. When he was CEO, he could not sleep at night if someone else offered a better value on a product. He cared deeply about how employees were treated, and he refused to accept a salary comparable to other CEOs in the industry. He also has nothing to do with Costco book sales, nor would he wish to at this point. We have much common ground and are friends, even though we often discuss political issues.

There is no need for political differences to precipitate hostility in personal relationships. We can build a strong, prosperous nation together if we are willing to talk and use our collective strengths to accomplish common goals. We must maintain open channels of communication, and as a society, we must learn to vote wisely with both the ballot and the wallet.

~~~

Rudderless U.S. Foreign Policy

July 30, 2014

The Obama administration's recent failures in the foreign-policy arena have only highlighted how far American leadership has fallen in this new century. From the Middle East to Eurasia, it often seems that President Obama is reacting to events instead of trying to shape them. Americans have begun to see his collective failures as an indictment on his presidency, and they long for clarity and purpose from their president.

The clear foreign policy that is grounded in American ideas of promoting liberty abroad and preserving our security at home is what is needed now. That is how we became a superpower. Reversing these ideas allows our adversaries to become stronger and impairs our ability to respond to present-day threats.

While Obama's foreign-policy adventures have waxed and waned in the eyes of the American public, his indecisiveness in places such as Iraq and Syria has presented an image of weakness on the global stage.

We have failed to adequately deal with Russian aggression in Georgia and Ukraine. Recognizing that the United States would soon be changing administrations, Russia invaded Georgia in 2008. As a nation, we stood by and watched during that transition, as parts of Georgia fell under Russian rule. Vladimir Putin sensed our weakness and saw opportunity. Six years later, he annexed Crimea, and now pro-Russian forces are trying to take over more land in Ukraine.

What has the Obama administration done in response to this aggression by Russia? Not really much, other than impose toothless sanctions on Russian businessmen close to Putin (but not the Russian president himself), which have done little to make Russia change course. Is this what Ronald Reagan would have done? Or would he have helped pro-democracy Ukrainians and pressed Europe to look for alternatives to Russian natural gas to preclude being held hostage by Russian energy? Additionally, we need to reinforce our commitments to NATO and get the former components of the Soviet Union involved. Otherwise, Putin will do this again. We need to embolden Europe to confront him.

Russia is not the only country that has taken advantage of our preoccupation with the Middle East. Recently, China has been expanding its maritime boundary in the South China Sea. It also seeks to test our resolve to long-held security commitments we have with our partners in Asia. We must do more to let our Asian allies know that we will stand with them and confront China's territorial ambitions. China continues to threaten our country with cyber-attacks and is a repressive global power. We need to do more to support those people in China who long for democratic reform.

If we had supported the masses who were trying to overthrow the tyrannical government in Iran in 2009, I suspect we would be looking at a very different situation in the Middle East today. The United States should always stand on the side of freedom-loving people. What has the Obama administration done to support those who long for liberty and freedom in Iran? More needs to be done.

Our foreign policy is rudderless. We are a ship lost at sea. We need a foreign policy that is proactive in safeguarding our interests and not reactive to events unfolding around the globe that affect our security. Our friends and allies need to know that we can be counted on when they are in jeopardy or when their security is threatened. We must have a foreign policy that is rooted in those ideas that have made us the envy of all freedom-loving people around the globe.

~~~

The Spreading Scourge of Anti-Christian Persecution

August 6, 2014

Intolerance that fosters pogroms abroad is taking root in U.S. communities. Sobering and unforgettable images are projected across our television and computer screens. They should elicit the most basic instincts of both fear and compassion.

I'm referring to images of showing the persecution of hundreds of thousands, perhaps even millions, of our fellow brothers and sisters by incomprehensible religious zealots. Their intolerance of Christianity is beyond horrible. People are beheaded for their faith. Women and young girls are sexually violated, and whole families are wantonly slaughtered in cold blood. Perhaps just as abhorrent is the profound silence of the current administration. Even though President Obama has declared that we are not a Judeo-Christian nation, we are still compassionate people who should not ignore humanitarian atrocities, much less ones where the victims are only guilty of maintaining a belief in the principles espoused by Jesus Christ.

We have an obligation as Americans to denounce these acts of persecution. Even those who do not worship a higher deity should be concerned. For when we stand up to such intolerance, we are defending the root of freedom. We are defending choice -- the ability to worship and call on the name of a heavenly being without fear of torture and abandonment.

The president, who very early in his tenure won the Nobel Peace Prize, now has an opportunity to truly be the broker of peace in a very troubled part of the world. He can be a champion of freedom of religion, a founding principle of our nation. As long as religious practices do not infringe upon the rights of others, he can make it clear that it is wrong to interfere with those practices.

In our own country, we must become more reasonable in disputes about religious symbols. For instance, if a Christmas tree or manger scene has been a long-standing community tradition, and a few offended people come along and claim that it must be removed, should those few individuals have the power to interfere with the seasonal joy of thousands who rejoice in the viewing of those symbols? If someone is offended by a menorah in a Jewish community, would it not make more sense to give them sensitivity training rather than disturb the entire community by removing the symbol? I could go on, but I think the point is clear. When we reward unwarranted hypersensitivity surrounding religious ceremonies or beliefs, we add fuel to the hatred and intolerance that subsequently produces religious persecution.

Some will say religious persecution in other parts of the world does not concern us and we cannot be the police for the planet. Certainly, there is some validity to the latter part of that statement, but if we continue to ignore or tolerate religious persecution elsewhere, it is just a matter of time before we will experience it here at home.

As far as the Middle East is concerned, we are not helpless and can dispatch the State Department to do all it can to help. Some conservatives and cynics might argue that such a move requires government dollars. Who's to say? We don't fully comprehend how besieged these people are, much less know what it would take to grant them relief.

Governments need to decry such persecution, and root it out wherever and whenever they can. The United States should lead in that effort -- just as it has with combating sex trafficking and other problems the world has decried in the past. It is hard to find an issue that demands a sharper clarion call for leadership now.

~~~

The Patriotism of Prosperity

August 13, 2014

A few weeks ago, it was quite revealing -- but not surprising -- to hear Treasury Secretary Jacob Lew imply that corporate America should willingly pay the highest corporate-tax rates in the world as part of its "patriotic" duty. This kind of discourse demonstrates a profound misunderstanding of capitalism, which is an important component of American exceptionalism.

In our system, people do not go into business, in many cases risking everything they have and more, in order to support the government. They obviously take those kinds of risks to make money. Instead of chastising American businesses for making financially prudent overseas investments, a wise and understanding government would be creating a domestic environment that is conducive to investment, innovation and growth, reducing the appeal of foreign explorations. A fair tax structure and a reduction in unnecessary regulations would go a long way toward establishing this environment.

Recently, President Obama indicated displeasure with the large and very successful medical-device company Medtronic, which has made public plans to acquire the Dublin-based company Covidien. This would result in one of the largest tax-inversion deals in history. Medtronic would move its headquarters from Minnesota to Ireland, relinquishing some of its American identity but reaping massive tax benefits because they would be taxed at the Irish corporate rate rather than the American corporate rate.

In a recent West Coast speech, Obama said companies doing such things are "technically renouncing their U.S. citizenship." He added, referring to such companies, "You don't get to pick which tax rate you pay." The fact is, they do get to pick their rate, because they are mobile and not yet under the complete control of a tyrannical government.

The days of an insular business environment are long gone from America, and we must recognize that we are players on the global stage. This means successful businesses will take advantage of conditions anywhere in the world that will promote their growth and value to shareholders. Instead of patriotism being defined as unthinking devotion to governmental tax edicts, perhaps it is better described as using one's talents and resources to bring strength and prosperity to our land through the successful utilization of advantages found worldwide. Our tax and regulatory policies should be aimed at helping companies achieve this latter definition.

Many American companies have social-responsibility committees that are very popular with socially conscious directors. They commit time, effort and money to enhancing the quality of life in their local communities, as well as nationally and globally. By not punishing these companies with corporate-tax rates that no other country in the world sees as reasonable, we not only contribute to their financial well-being, but we also greatly enhance their ability to have a positive effect on social problems here in the United States.

There is absolutely no need for animosity between the government and business. When businesses are successful, the reservoirs from which taxes are paid are much larger, resulting in more money for the government even though tax rates would be lower. If we enact policies that allow American companies to bring back hundreds of billions of dollars in corporate profits to our country without punitive taxation, the upside would be considerably greater than any negative consequences. This is not complex economic theory; it's common sense.

As the president and Congress consider enacting regulations to limit or eliminate future inversion deals, I hope they take the time to talk to a wide spectrum of business leaders about ways to create a fertile and friendly atmosphere for innovation and growth. It will require more than just talk to persuade American companies to stay or return to our shores. Instead of just talking about fixing our taxation woes, we need to just do it. And I hope grateful companies will feel an obligation to do even more to contribute to the well-being of the citizens of our nation.

~~~

Forgetting the Meaning of Freedom

August 20, 2014

Many people in this country were shocked when the U.S. Navy recently announced the removal of all Bibles from military hotels under their control. This was in response to pressure from the Freedom From Religion Foundation, a well-known atheist group.

The surprise is not the hypocritical stance of the Freedom From Religion Foundation, but rather the fact that an established bulwark of American strength and patriotism caved to a self-serving group of religious fanatics. The previous sentence may seem out of place if you don't realize that atheism is actually a religion.

Like traditional religions, atheism requires strong conviction. In the case of atheists, it's the belief that there is no God and that all things can be proved by science. It is extremely hypocritical of the foundation to request the removal of Bibles from hotel rooms on the basis of their contention that the presence of Bibles indicates that the government is choosing one religion over another. If they really thought about it, they would realize that removal of religious materials imposes their religion on everyone else.

Some atheists argue that there should be a library or cachet of religious material at the check-in desk of a hotel from which any guest could order a Bible, Torah or Koran for their reading pleasure. No favoritism would be shown through such a system, and those who reject the idea of God would not have to be offended.

This is like saying there shouldn't be certain brands of bottled water in hotel rooms because there may be guests who prefer a different type of water or are offended by bottled water and think everybody should be drinking tap water. The logical answer to such absurdity would, of course, be that the offended individual could bring his own water or simply ignore the brand of water he does not care for.

As a nation, we must avoid the paralysis of hypersensitivity, which prevents us from getting anything done because virtually everything offends someone. We need to distribute "big boy" pants to help the whiners learn to focus their energy in a productive way. We must also go back and read the Constitution, including the First Amendment, which guarantees freedom of religion. It says nothing about freedom from religion, and in fact, if you consider the context and the lives of those involved in the crafting of our founding documents, it is apparent that they believed in allowing their faith to guide their lives. This has nothing to do with imposing one's beliefs on someone else.

Those of us who do believe in God can hope and pray that at some point secular progressives will come to understand that they must abide by the same rules with which they attempt to control others. There is nothing wrong with the philosophy of "live and let live." America was designed to be a free country, where people could live as they pleased and pursue their dreams as long as they didn't infringe upon the rights of others. By continually broadening the scope of an "infringement" on the rights of others, the purveyors of division will succeed in destroying our nation -- but only if we continue to cater to their divisive rhetoric.

Liberty and justice for all has worked extremely well for an extended period of time, and there is no reason to upset the equilibrium by endowing the hypersensitive complainers in our society with more power than everyone else. Thankfully, the Navy quickly realized its mistake and restored the Bible to its lodges. Maybe now we can deal with the real issues that threaten our safety.

~~~

A Problem Bigger than Ferguson

August 27, 2014

The international spotlight has recently been shining on Ferguson, Mo., after an 18-year-old black man was fatally shot by a white police officer. There was massive national and international media coverage, much of it engendered by the tantalizing thought that here was a clear-cut case of racism leading to police brutality and indicative of the evil inherent in American society. Violent demonstrations and riots ensued, with massive property damage and many outside agitators descending on the town, supposedly to guarantee justice as defined by mob mentality.

Perhaps it would be useful to examine the tragedy with the facts on the table rather than through the lenses of hypersensitized emotions stimulated by those attempting to exploit the situation.

Michael Brown was 6-foot-4 and 290 pounds. He had marijuana in his system and was purportedly involved in a strong-arm robbery prior to the shooting. He and a companion were walking in the middle of the street and obstructing traffic and therefore were admonished by a police officer to move to the sidewalk. Brown, who may have been pharmacologically impaired, became belligerent, and the ensuing struggle produced facial trauma and an orbital fracture of the police officer's face. The officer, who may have been dazed by a blow to the cranium severe enough to produce a fracture, attempted to apprehend the assailant, and shots were fired, six of which struck the suspect, resulting in a fatality.

Regardless of one's position on the political spectrum, we can all agree that this was a horrible tragedy and needless discarding of a precious life. How could this have been avoided? Two obvious answers: The officer could have ignored his duty and backed off when it became apparent that his instructions would not be followed, thereby avoiding a confrontation, or Brown could have complied with the officer's instructions, according to his civic duties.

If police officers generally adopted the first solution, chaos would reign supreme in all of our streets. If the populace generally adopted the second solution, there would be even fewer incidents of police violence. Last year, 100 black males were killed by police in the United States. In the same year, 5,000 blacks were killed by other blacks, the vast majority being males. Could it be that we are erroneously being manipulated into making this incident a racial issue, when, in fact, it is a component of a much larger social issue?

Why are there so many young black men in the streets of America with defiant attitudes that frequently lead to incarceration or death? Could it be that a large number of them grow up without a father figure to teach them how to relate to authority and the meaning of personal responsibility? This is not to say that mothers cannot convey these important social lessons, as mine did. But in too many cases, these young unwed mothers have never themselves been exposed to personal responsibility and self-esteem, and the vicious cycle continues. As a society, we must concentrate on ways to break this tragic cycle that has produced a higher poverty rate in black communities across America with the increasing frustrations that underscore potentially explosive, tinderbox situations, as we have seen in Ferguson.

Once we get the most powerful economic engine the world has ever seen back on track with sensible economic policies, we should devote some of the tax revenues generated to child-care facilities that would allow many of those unwed mothers to get their General Education Development or higher degree and become self-supporting. There are also a number of programs across the nation that offer free classes that teach social and job skills, which would give many of the young men some different options.

We must concentrate on these kinds of programs because we cannot afford to lose large segments of our society to despair and underachievement in an increasingly competitive world. We have a social crisis brewing if we continue down the path we are on now, but we have the power to change our downward course with true compassion that allows people to rise and escape dependency.

~~~

Resisting the Islamic State's Demand for Submission

September 3, 2014

The Islamic State and the other advocates of Shariah law are growing rapidly, along with their zeal to eradicate or convert all "infidels." For those who are asleep at the wheel, in the opinion of these fanatics, most of Western civilization -- including America -- fits into the infidel category.

I normally encourage conversation and compromise where possible, but how does one negotiate or compromise with someone who desires your elimination? Maybe if you meet some of their demands, they will only dismember you or kill you more slowly.

Obviously, the expansion of groups like the Islamic State represents an existential threat to our own nation and our way of life. If ever there was a time to work together for self-preservation, it is now. There really is no time to squabble about who was right and who was wrong regarding our activities in the Middle East. Our enemies will use every opportunity to divide us and distract us, which will make their job of destroying us much easier.

In order to prevail in the war on terror, we must have an overall strategy, the goal of which is annihilation of the terrorists, as opposed to simply winning battles with them here and there. This means paying much more attention to military preparedness, both offensive and defensive. That means significantly increasing our covert operations, without blabbing to the world about what we will or will not do. It means cultivating strong and trusting relationships with our allies and never leaving them to worry about abandonment for political reasons. It means helping other countries in the region to realize that they, too, will soon be targets of the Islamic State, which will radically alter their comfortable lives.

When it comes to the elimination of those trying to destroy us, we have to be smart enough to realize that we must have airtight borders to prevent easy access for terrorists. Some say this is too difficult. I guarantee that it is easier than trying to rebuild a nation that has been destroyed because we thought logical defense was too hard. There is no question that unpleasantries brought about by our own forces will be necessary to accomplish our goals and defeat terrorism, but you cannot win a politically correct war.

Our enemies' desire to establish a caliphate is no joke. Their convert-or-die doctrine parallels some of the social philosophies enforced by the political-correctness police in this country. Either you accept their interpretation of what is moral and correct, or the name calling starts, and they attempt to destroy your business or reputation.

We despise the Islamic State, but do not see the same ugliness in our own tactics. The truth hurts, and it is much easier to ignore it or try to demonize its bearer. Unless integrity, courage and common sense result in the ability to honestly examine our own hypocrisy, we will lose the war of ideas and identity, and the land of the free will become a distant memory.

I've been privileged to get to know some incredibly smart and talented military leaders, as well as covert operators and innovative engineers. I am confident that with our talent and faith, not only can we win this war, but we can show the world a better way.

~~~

Ray Rice's Crime and Punishment, with Compassion

September 10, 2014

The incident in which Baltimore Ravens running back Ray Rice savagely beat his fiancee in an elevator has garnered much attention, largely because the savagery was captured on video.

The video evoked a visceral response in almost everyone, present company included. To brutally attack someone you supposedly love with enough force to threaten her life is very abnormal behavior. If the perpetrator is simply punished and the behavior not addressed, it is likely to manifest again, perhaps with even more serious consequences. Of course punishment for this heinous act is warranted. But where would any of us be if, after we committed some terrible act, everyone just piled on and no one sought to help us?

Having been the transgressor as a teenager and almost stabbing someone, and subsequently by the grace of God learning how to look at things differently and resolve conflict without violence, I came to understand rage, consequences, penalties and redemption. Perhaps we should all take a step back from our pedestals of righteousness and let rational thought processes have a place in our lives.

The point is, let's not get into useless discussions of whether Rice's punishment is not severe enough or too severe, because that is probably pointless. Instead, let's get help for these people and engage in useful dialogue about the horrors of domestic violence. Then, hopefully, we can use this as a teachable moment.

Undoubtedly, those on the left will say Rice's abominable actions are being defended by Ben Carson, who thinks domestic violence is not so bad. This is nothing more than the usual superficial, desperate attempts to diminish someone they are worried about and for whom they have no good arguments.

I would happily engage in a public debate with any of my left-wing critics on the issue of domestic violence, punishment and rehabilitation. We might even be able to reach some common ground and make progress if we stop using every opportunity to stoke the fires of hypersensitivity and division in our society. To even suggest that an intelligent person would defend the actions of Rice or blame his fiancee for the crime is beyond ludicrous. However, if there were not an appetite for such idiocy, it wouldn't exist.

There are some who will say that Rice was defending himself from his fiancee, who was attacking him. He is so much bigger and stronger than she is that he easily could have restrained her without striking her. There is no excuse for pummeling anyone, much less a smaller, weaker individual.

Many have been quick to jump to the conclusion that his fiancee, who is now his wife, was only in the relationship for the money, and there is no possibility that love enters the equation. This may or may not be the case, but it is a private matter for the Rice family to resolve on their own. Hopefully, that resolution will involve much-needed counseling to uncover the root causes of their problems. If they can go on to lead successful and happy lives even without the NFL, they will have achieved a good outcome.

~~~

A Plea for Constitutional Literacy on this Constitution Day

September 17, 2014

Earlier this summer, I managed to perplex, perhaps even offend, a famous TV interviewer when I declared I want a federal government that follows the U.S. Constitution. Seemingly aghast, the interviewer went so far as to suggest my position was a "highly charged thing to say."

Imagine that. A journalist -- who, owing to the Constitution, has the right to report and speak freely -- being uncomfortable with a fellow American's allegiance to the Constitution and to the Founding Fathers' vision of a limited central government.

I fear we as a nation have drifted too far away from an understanding and appreciation of the greatest governance document the world has ever produced. We have a president today who usurps power never given to him in the Constitution, a dysfunctional Congress so gridlocked that it can't fulfill its mission as a separate-but-equal branch of government, and a Fourth Estate of media elites who cheerlead for a bigger, more intrusive government that unnecessarily addicts those struggling to escape poverty to handouts, rather than encouraging self-reliance.

Let me be clear. Rightly sized and empowered, government serves an excellent purpose. Our Founding Fathers knew that and created a perfect vision for a republic of independent states protected and served by a central federal government with strong checks and balances. Those checks on powers were essential to the Framers, who established three equal but separate branches to ensure we always had a government "of the people, for the people and by the people," as Abraham Lincoln so wisely said.

But today we have people who are simply overgoverned -- subjected to taxation, regulation and intrusions by a massive federal government that our Founding Fathers never would have tolerated. It wants to control what we eat, how we live and even how much we can earn. It values political correctness over freedom, codependence over self-reliance, and redistribution of wealth over personal success.

That's why I said what I did that Sunday morning to that talk-show host. I told him I would love to have a government again that places the Constitution at the center of its mission, that recognizes government was never intended to intrude on every aspect of our lives. Everywhere I go in this great nation these days, I hear that same plea, from farmers in rural communities fearful the next federal regulation will put their generations-old family farm out of business, to shopkeepers suffocating under an unnecessarily high tax burden, to young people seemingly reconciled that their government will monitor, record and track their every movement.

How do we reverse this creeping despair that we have drifted too far away from our founding principles? It's simple. I think we must go back to the source of our great American experiment: the U.S. Constitution.

In little more than 4,500 words, the Framers created a vision of government that preserves liberty first and foremost and also serves the basic needs of a republic. For 200 years, that document has guided this great nation through dark times and soaring success. For most of our history, schoolchildren were taught the guiding principles of the Constitution from the earliest age, and even members of Congress with controversial civil rights histories such as the late Sen. Strom Thurmond of South Carolina and Sen. Robert Byrd of West Virginia kept a copy of that great document in their jacket pockets to remind them of the responsibilities and limits of governance.

On this Constitution Day, a wonderful holiday created with bipartisan support just a few short years ago, let's recommit ourselves to rereading and appreciating our Constitution and to ensuring that our children and our children's children grow up with the same appreciation we were given. Familiarity with the greatest ideas ever created for preserving liberty will breed appreciation. Appreciation will help us all overcome the ignorant political correctness of a few media elites and governing officials who seem to dismiss the fundamental principles of a government that respects liberty first and foremost.

~~~

Courage Learned in Classrooms and at Kitchen Tables Can Thwart Despair

September 24, 2014

We have heard much about the tragic events in Ferguson, Mo., during which a young man lost his life, a community became enraged and many differing definitions of justice emerged. All human life is precious, and we should be concerned when any life is prematurely terminated, regardless of the circumstances. If we as a society could focus the same kind of attention on the everyday murderous carnage that threatens the vitality of many of our cities, perhaps some meaningful solutions could be found.

Growing up in inner-city America, I witnessed many instances of premature death, usually inflicted by other inner-city residents. I also witnessed many stories of triumph that produced successful individuals out of the same environment. Perhaps it would be worthwhile to study the factors that led to success instead of tragedy in the same environment. Obviously, volumes have been written about this topic, on which many consider themselves experts. In many cases, the observations and analyses are accurate and thought-provoking, and in many cases, they are cowardly and pandering.

There is a long list of factors highly correlated with success regardless of the environment. They include strong supportive families, a sense of personal responsibility, good role models, faith that produces a sense of purpose and values, hard work, confidence, courage, an emphasis on education, and caring neighbors. As many who have read some of my books know, I have written volumes on all of these topics, and all are deserving of much attention, but in this limited article, I will focus on the last three.

We live in an increasingly technical world, where knowledge is power. Even in an economy that is stagnant, it is still relatively easy to obtain a good job when one has acquired the requisite knowledge and skills. Many sophisticated jobs go begging or have to be filled by foreigners because we are not producing technical graduates in sufficient numbers. We must also look at successful educational models, including charter schools, and insist that they be made available to inner-city students. There are a number of excellent reading-room programs throughout the country that incentivize students, particularly from Title I schools, to learn to enjoy reading, which profoundly decreases the dropout rate later on. Lack of education in this country is a major barrier between the haves and the have-nots, and we must concentrate on it.

I remember as a child referring to some of the older neighbors as crotchety and mean because they never let us get away with wrongdoing. We thought they should mind their own business, and I even remember some instances where their windows would be purposely broken. In retrospect, they were the very ones who kept us out of trouble, and obviously, they usually cared deeply about our welfare. The me-first mentality that has infected our society, along with the fear of retribution, has largely extinguished these kinds of neighbors in many cities today. Given the level of violence, one can hardly blame people for keeping their mouths shut, but we must also realize that if we don't nip bad behavior in the bud, it only grows, creating more intimidation, and the vicious cycle continues.

Courage from the kitchen table, the pulpit, the classroom and the streets was prevalent when I was a child. Many people had no problem publicly denouncing deleterious behavior even if it made them temporarily unpopular. Fear of being called names or being proclaimed out of touch has paralyzed many in our inner cities, just as it has throughout the nation. We must realize that we are all in the same boat, and we can sink together in the quagmire of fractious accusations and hatred, or we can rise together to previously unexperienced heights if we learn from past mistakes and embrace the principles that created, in record time, the greatest nation in history.

~~~

Americans Have a Civic Duty To Vote Intelligently

October 1, 2014

Many recent surveys indicate that the vast majority of Americans feel our country is moving in the wrong direction.

This country was intentionally designed to be different from others in which a monarch or strong central government controlled almost every aspect of the lives of its citizens. In most other nations, the lives of the populace conform to the will of the government. In America, the government is supposed to conform to the will of the people. Also in most other countries, it was declared that the rights of the people were conferred by the government; whereas, our founding documents indicate a belief that our rights derive from our Creator, a.k.a. God.

It is critical that the people of our country understand that we the people are at the pinnacle of power in a nation created of, by and for the people. In order to exercise that power in a responsible manner, the people must be informed voters. To cast votes for people or issues about which one knows little or nothing is akin to taking unlabeled medicine from an unknown source simply because someone told you to do so.

It is also unfortunate that many schools no longer offer civics courses and that students are not taught the fundamentals of how our government works. This partly explains the incredibly uninformed answers to basic questions on some televised "man on the street" interviews. The founders of our nation were huge advocates of education and felt that our freedoms and system of government would be jeopardized by an uninformed populace that could be easily manipulated by dishonest politicians or a biased press.

I hate to complain without offering solutions. Thus, my wife and I have just released a new e-book (soon to be a paperback) titled, "One Vote: Make Your Voice Heard." Thousands of free copies are being distributed, and the purchase price is less than that of a simple sandwich. It is completely nonpartisan and was written for people who, for whatever reason, missed out on important information with respect to becoming an informed voter. There are electronic links to websites that not only identify your representatives, but also tell you how they voted, as opposed to how they said they voted, on a variety of issues. It provides access to links that help you clearly identify your own beliefs and compare them with those of political figures and parties. This kind of information will make it easier for people to think for themselves, rather than being herded and manipulated by those in various political organizations who hunger for power, not liberty and fairness.

In 2012, 93 million Americans who could have voted failed to do so. That's more votes than either presidential candidate received. We must all realize that we have no right to complain about the direction of our nation if we are unwilling to grasp the importance of our civic duty to vote intelligently.

There are those who are much more interested in having blind followers than informed voters. They will not embrace this publication. I also fully realize that detractors will say Ben Carson is just engaging in self-promotion and trying to make more money. Some people ascribe to others what their motives would be and are incapable of thinking otherwise. In the meantime, we the people must, through our collective wisdom and power, alter the course of our beloved nation through the wise use of our votes.

~~~

Keep Ebola Out of America

October 8, 2014

As the Ebola infection rate and death toll continue to rise rapidly on the African continent, many of us have become complacent with the measures we have taken to protect Americans from this deadly disease.

Other nations, such as England, have gone so far as to ban flights emanating from the affected regions of Africa. The Centers for Disease Control and various infectious-disease specialists have done a yeoman's job in their efforts to prevent infected individuals in our country from contaminating others. They have put excellent protocols in place that would virtually guarantee complete safety. Unfortunately, all of those valiant efforts cannot preclude human error, which remains an ever-present danger, regardless of intellect.

For this reason, I and many others are not comfortable with the idea of bringing infected individuals into our midst when we can readily treat them elsewhere and happily receive them back once the infectious danger has passed.

When one does a logical benefit-to-risk analysis, it is clear that the worst things that could happen by intentionally bringing this dangerous disease to America are far worse than the best things that could happen. Some say if we bring infected individuals here, it will accelerate research endeavors and a potential cure or effective vaccination. Others say not bringing infected citizens back demonstrates an insensitivity toward wonderful people who risk their lives for others. I am sympathetic to these arguments, and if we did not have safer alternatives, they would convince me.

Perhaps we should be concentrating on stopping the spread of Ebola in Africa and eradicating it from Earth. Like the war on terrorism, we should fight it elsewhere to decrease the likelihood of needing to fight it here. African lives are every bit as valuable as lives in America or anywhere else, and this humanitarian crisis has enormous health implications for the whole world. If, as some officials say, bringing infected individuals back here expedites the acquisition of knowledge that could lead to a cure, as all components of the disease could be more carefully studied, why not transport more researchers and facilities to the heart of the epidemic and dramatically accelerate the process?

I have no desire to induce panic, but we must realize that some viruses are known to undergo mutations that make them even more virulent. If the Ebola virus becomes even more pathologic, the ensuing panic and destruction of human life could go far beyond what is currently being acknowledged. This means there is some urgency to getting the outbreak in Africa under control.

The point is, this is an extremely dangerous disease with the potential to spread throughout several African countries and, subsequently, into other parts of the world, including the United States. Most crises prompt warnings, which, if heeded and acted upon, can avert disaster. On the other hand, if arrogance and mistakes characterize the response, horrendous results are likely to ensue.

If we stop trying to prove we are right -- whatever our opinions are -- and instead concentrate our efforts on halting the spread of the disease where it is concentrated and finding a cure, perhaps we could avert needless panic and death throughout Africa, America and the world.

~~~

Americans, Like the Founders, Must Gather the Courage that Forged a Nation

October 15, 2014

It should come as no surprise to most thinking people that Wal-Mart, like many other large employers, recently announced it would be suspending health-care benefits for part-time workers. This is really a double hit on workers: In many cases, they previously had full-time jobs with 40-hour workweeks before being reduced to part-time status and now losing their health benefits.

The "Affordable Care Act," which probably seems less affordable to most Americans as we find out more about it, is the cause of this unnecessary misery. When the employer mandate, which is part of Obamacare, is activated early next year, tens of millions more Americans will face dramatic hikes in the cost of the health care they currently receive or will lose it altogether. The current administration understood that this would happen, which occasioned the issuing of several executive orders delaying the implementation of the employer mandate until after the November 2014 elections.

The thing that is most disturbing to me about this government-manufactured attack on the well-being of hardworking American citizens is the apparent contempt for the intelligence of the American populace. These kinds of maneuvers assume that many citizens are not bright enough to realize they are being manipulated politically and that things that impact them so negatively are being pushed off until after an election, when they willingly give their votes to the very people who are using them.

The same slick politicians who convinced large portions of the populace that Obamacare would be the panacea for all of their medical needs, and that you could keep your doctor and your insurance if you were satisfied with them, also told us that the IRS scandal was phony and that pertinent records and emails coincidentally disappeared from the computers of the main people under suspicion. They also want people to believe the tragedy in Benghazi was the result of an inflammatory video and that anyone questioning the veracity of such a scenario is clearly a partisan troublemaker who dislikes the current administration.

The list of problems is too long for this article, but any objective individual would not have a difficult time understanding that Americans are faced with a less than honest government, as well as a press that has forgotten why it is protected by the First Amendment. The Founders envisioned the press as an ally of the people, rather than an arm of a political ideology. All of us, including the press, must learn the difference between policies that are pro-America and anti-America, and to recognize those that are meant to benefit a particular party.

This situation leaves "we the people" with an incredibly important choice regarding our relationship with those who govern us. We can go along to get along and make sure that no one calls us a nasty name or challenges our comfort -- or, like the patriots who preceded us, we can embrace the values and principles that once gave us a strong identity as a "can-do nation" with strong faith and compassion.

Those are the values that allowed a ragtag army during the American Revolution to defeat the most powerful military force on Earth. They did not possess a superior fighting force or ingenious strategies, but they did hold strong beliefs, for which they were willing to die, while the British soldiers were just following orders. That same kind of conviction today could lead us to become informed voters and exercise the powers vested in us courageously.

Historically, during great cultural clashes, those with strong convictions and beliefs have overcome those with weak convictions, who have lost their identity. We are now involved in a worldwide conflict with forces that wish to destroy America and our way of life. We can capitulate to the forces of political correctness and surrender everything that made us strong and unique for the sake of not offending anyone, or we can proudly embrace the values and principles that made us great, honor our Constitution and place our trust in God. This is our best safeguard.

~~~

Houston's First Amendment Problem

October 22, 2014

The recent questionably unconstitutional moves by the Houston city council to subpoena the sermons of five area ministers, as well as internal correspondence dealing with social issues, should have the American Civil Liberties Union and everyone else who believes in free speech and religious freedom up in arms.

We as Americans must guard every aspect of our Constitution and recognize when it is being threatened. One of the great dangers in America today is extreme intolerance in the name of tolerance.

For example, in this Houston case, it is presupposed that the pastors in question may have said something that was objectionable to the homosexual community. In order to prove that we are tolerant of the homosexual lifestyle, we as a society allow gays to be intolerant of anyone who disagrees with them in any way.

Of course, gays should be able to live in any manner they choose as long as it does not infringe on the rights of anyone else. And of course, ministers should be able to preach according to the dictates of their conscience as long as they are not forcing others to listen. This concept of "live and let live" is an essential ingredient of harmonious living in a diverse society. We cannot single out the side we want to castigate for intolerance while letting the other side get away with it without comment.

Perhaps it is time for Americans to take an honest look at what it means to live peacefully in a diverse society composed of people with many different points of view. This requires true tolerance, which includes being capable of listening to people with views that might differ from yours.

Many of us who are Christians have strong beliefs that inform our thinking on many issues, but in no way should those beliefs lead us to demonize or treat others unfairly. The same applies to Muslims, Jews, every other religious group and atheists. When our universities attempt to shield students from hearing the opinions of those with whom the administration disagrees, they are not only being intolerant, but are teaching the next generation those same destructive ideas that will eventually dissolve the cohesiveness of our society and lead to our downfall.

Perhaps a dose of maturity on all sides would put an end to the mindless name-calling and baseless accusations against those with whom we disagree and instead lead to constructive civil discourse. After all, it often is easier to learn from those with whom we disagree than from those with whom we always agree. Also, conversation erases many misconceptions that drive hatred. That is the reason famed community organizer Saul Alinsky, in his book "Rules for Radicals," stated that you should never have a conversation with your adversaries, because that humanizes them, and your job is to demonize them. When your agenda is to fundamentally change a society, it is a much easier task when you stifle conversation and debate.

Our Founders were very concerned about free speech and religious freedom because they came from countries where these basic elements of American life were compromised. The First Amendment to the Constitution was carefully crafted to preclude the imposition of laws and ordinances that trample on these rights. The Houston issue goes far beyond free speech and homosexual rights. It warns us of what can happen if we are not vigilant in guarding our hard-fought freedoms. Fortunately, a firestorm of immediate protests appears to have at least temporarily rolled back this egregious assault on all Americans, whether they realize it or not.

We can never allow civil authorities to censor or control the content of religious sermons, or we will eventually become a completely different country with far fewer rights than we currently enjoy. Freedom is not free, and those who do not zealously guard it will lose it.

~~~

America's Most Incurable Disease Is Spending

October 29, 2014

I have had a fulfilling career as a pediatric neurosurgeon, which unfortunately included numerous instances where worst-case scenarios played out in the operating room. Good surgeons plan ahead for these possible events so that bad outcomes are minimized. But of course, few treatment plans will succeed if the doctor continually fails to make a proper diagnosis before surgery begins.

When I look at our nation's massive federal debt, it is clear that Washington has chronically misdiagnosed the situation, which has resulted in a seemingly never-ending cycle of borrowing and spending. Much like a life-threatening disease, if the underlying cause is left unaddressed, patient recovery seldom occurs.

Bold leaders in both parties have warned for years that entitlement spending is the major driver of unsustainable deficits, and they have further advised that Washington implement policies to address this problem. While it is distressing to see continued inaction, what troubles me more is that virtually no one has addressed the underlying cause. In other words, why were programs created in a manner that they would eventually become so financially upside-down that our entire economy would be in jeopardy? Furthermore, can and should we do something to ensure that future entitlement programs are created carefully and responsibly?

Let's look at recent history. In the past 10 years, projected deficits for entitlements created long ago, such as Social Security and Medicare, have grown dramatically. In fact, existing entitlement programs consume about 60 percent of all federal spending. During this time, much political effort has been expended -- unsuccessfully -- trying to reform these programs. I'm not saying this wasn't an important effort. But, if these programs are not reformed soon, they will consume 100 percent of projected federal revenue within the next three decades. Imagine that: Our children and grandchildren either will be faced with a federal government that has no money for defense, roads and education, or the tax burden will double on citizens.

Sadly, while Congress was busy failing to fix these existing problems, it passed two new entitlement programs, both of which will only worsen our budgetary shortfalls. These programs create permanent commitments by the federal government to provide expensive services to people indefinitely, regardless of whether the nation can afford to do so. So, not only have we failed to stop the bleeding, but we also have managed to cause significantly more.

Setting aside the political debate about these two programs -- one passed by Democrats, the other by Republicans -- are any of us comfortable with the notion that permanent spending programs that grow on autopilot forever can be created as easily as Congress names a post office -- by a simple one-vote majority? I understand allowing Congress to pass bills with simple majorities that benefit current constituents, but shouldn't a bill that is going to affect generations to come require a greater threshold than a short-term partisan majority of as small as one single vote? Shouldn't such grant programs require greater debate, more bipartisanship, some level of consensus and, of course, fiscal responsibility? Absolutely.

Fortunately, there are some in Congress with real solutions. Rep. Rick Crawford, an Arkansas Republican, in conjunction with PreserveOurFuture.org, has properly diagnosed this problem and started crafting a superb treatment plan. They have proposed the Super Program Amendment, which would impose two new requirements: 1) a two-thirds majority vote to pass any new permanent entitlement program, and 2) no additional deficit spending for new entitlements created in the future. Imagine if such an amendment had been passed by Congress (and ratified by the states) as part of the budget reforms of the 1990s. Instead of seeing our unfunded obligations grow by tens of trillions of dollars, we would actually be in better financial health to deal with the unsustainable growth of entitlements today.

As a physician, I believe in prevention -- namely, taking those prudent steps now that can dramatically improve health down the road. The Super Program Amendment would ensure that short-term partisan majorities cannot do more harm to the fiscal health of our nation, giving us the time we need to find consensus on fixing the nation's other serious problems. Those problems affect everyone regardless of political affiliation, and we must all act as patriotic Americans to resolve them.

~~~

Phoning It In on Election Day: Too Many Americans Opt Out by Failing To Vote

November 5, 2014

With so much at stake, millions of Americans still did not participate in the midterm elections this week.

When the governing structure of our nation was put together, the Founders were excited about the prospect of a nation that placed the needs and desires of its citizens on a higher pedestal than those of the government itself. They also warned that it might be difficult to maintain such a government without it morphing into the usual "government knows best" model in place in most other countries of the world.

Some may think that a government that seldom interferes with the lives of its citizens and encourages entrepreneurship, growth, personal responsibility and independence is only wishful thinking and not practical. (They have resigned themselves to the ever increasing and controlling government we have now.) Nevertheless, the early years of America had such a government, and as a result, the nation rose from the habitat of an assorted group of courageous intellectuals supported by a ragtag militia in 1776 to the most dominant economic power in the world in less than 100 years.

What has created the malaise that characterizes so many potential American voters today? I have encountered hundreds of thousands of my fellow citizens on the road over the past year, and I have been struck by the level of animosity toward both major political parties and the feeling that nothing will improve -- regardless of which party is in power. There is also a massive lack of trust in our federal government, which greatly dampens enthusiasm for voter participation. Many others feel that their single vote means nothing. Therefore, exercising their civic responsibility is a waste of time.

The real question for conservatives after the gains they have made is whether they are going to put forth an aggressive agenda with the goals of spurring economic growth, reestablishing global leadership, and providing encouragement and mechanisms for the downtrodden to capitalize on the ideas of personal responsibility. They also should propose a well-defined and intelligible alternative to Obamacare, develop our abundant natural resources in an environmentally friendly way, and reform the monstrous tax code, among other things. Or are they simply going to try to block additional unconstitutional executive action and hope this will further endear them to the populace?

The problems we face are too serious and too numerous to put off addressing them until 2016. If we capitulate to frustration and tune out of the political process, we automatically further empower those who wish to fundamentally change our nation. Those of us with common sense and who love the values and principles that made us a great nation must not grow weary of the struggle that is required to ensure freedom and prosperity.

We must strive to re-involve the masses of our compatriots who have given up, using the promise of a nation where "we the people" compel the government through the political process in place to conform to our will. The next couple of years should be focused on citizen involvement and political activism in order to put forth a vision for our nation.

I don't blame my fellow citizens for being discouraged, given the radical changes that have been forced upon our society by a vocal minority with great political expertise. Let us use that discouragement as the impetus to discard the laissez-faire attitudes that have permitted these fundamental changes in our identity. In doing so, we can reclaim the zeal that characterized our predecessors, who persuaded those within their spheres of influence to actively participate in the shaping of a great nation.

~~~

A Common-Sense Prescription for Immigration Reform

November 12, 2014

We have all heard it said many times that America is a land of immigrants, some voluntary and some involuntary, but immigrants nevertheless. We have plenty of space in our country, but insufficient resources to support everyone who wants to come here. When we see innocent children used as political pawns, it still tugs at our heartstrings, which is the desired intent. The real question is: What are we going to do about it? Immigration reform has been a very tough issue, as well as a political football, and it has produced governmental stalemates and no useful solutions for decades.

President Obama's decision to act unilaterally outside of Congress is not the answer. Instead, Congress must use its lawmaking powers to fix a system that is so broken that only a legislative solution can fix it. The lack of policy progress has been incredibly frustrating, and the humanitarian border crisis this summer only highlighted how badly we need a system that deals efficiently and effectively with both illegal and legal immigration.

It is time for Congress to act and to do so in a bipartisan fashion that engenders the confidence of the American people. There are many common-sense prescriptions within reach of our government. It is time to seize them.

To begin to solve this problem, we must first have some understanding of why it exists. Despite all of its problems, America is still the place of dreams. As such, it is small wonder that so many from other nations would like to live here.

Right now, we have very porous borders and unenthusiastic and inconsistent enforcement of immigration laws. Further incentives for illegal immigration are easy enrollment in public schools, easy employment for those willing to take jobs others don't want, easy access to health care and easy acquisition of public support through welfare programs. Yet this population cannot participate in the formal workforce, which means they cannot contribute fully to their local economies.

Any discussion of immigration reform should include bipartisan solutions that both address the undocumented population here today and discourage illegal immigration going forward. If these issues are not addressed, solutions will fall short. On the other hand, if all of these issues are addressed firmly and consistently, we can uphold the rule of law and discourage further illegal immigration. Detractors will say that if it were that simple, it already would have been done and we wouldn't be having this discussion. What they fail to account for is the fact that the issues have not been addressed.

A national guest-worker program makes sense and seems to work well in Canada. Noncitizens would have to apply for a guest-worker permit and have a guaranteed job awaiting them. Taxes would be paid at a rate commensurate with other U.S. workers, and special visas would allow for easy entry and egress across borders. Guest-worker status would be granted to individuals and not to groups.

People already here illegally could apply for guest-worker status from outside of the country. This means they would have to leave first. They should in no way be rewarded for having broken our laws, but if they are wise, they will arrange with their employer before they leave to immediately offer them a legal job as soon as their application is received. When they return, they still would not be U.S. citizens, but they would be legal, and they would be paying taxes. Only jobs that are vacant as a result of a lack of interest by American citizens should be eligible for the guest-worker program.

In return for greater certainty on immigration, employers must bear some responsibility for making sure that no illegal immigrants are hired. Employers who break the rules should receive swift, severe and consistent punishment that constitutes a real deterrent and not a mere inconvenience. A second infraction should be a criminal offense and treated as such.

All of this is irrelevant unless we have secure borders. There is much that can be learned from security personnel in prisons and other secured facilities, and there is a great deal of smart technology that can be employed to achieve secure borders. It is a matter of will rather than ability.

As long as we reward people who break laws, they will continue to break laws. We do need a continual flow of immigrants, but choosers need not be beggars. We make decisions based on our needs. People who refuse to comply with the rules must forfeit chances of legalization in the future. Anyone caught involved in voter fraud should be immediately deported and have his citizenship revoked. The point is this: We must create a system that disincentivizes illegal immigration and upholds the rule of law while providing us with a steady stream of immigrants from other nations who will strengthen our society. Let's solve the problem and stop playing political football.

~~~

Stupidity Reconsidered: Election Proved Americans Aren't Fooled by Gruber and Obama

November 19, 2014

Jonathan Gruber set off a firestorm of controversy, at least in the conservative media, with the recent revelation of his comments about the "stupidity of the American people," which allowed the Affordable Care Act to be passed. In essence, he admitted that the bill was written in a way that would allow its purveyors to characterize it as the cure-all and salvation for a health care system that was in trouble, with no danger of their deception being discovered by a populace that is trusting and naive. He obviously never intended for his comments to make it into the public sphere and did not consider the fact that someone is always recording on their smartphone.

What is truly disturbing is the fact that our government is willing to engage in the purposeful deception of the populace in order to thrust its secretive agenda onto an unsuspecting populace and a sycophantic mainstream media. As I have said many times before, Obamacare was never about health care; it was about government control and wealth redistribution. If there was real concern about the uninsured, it would have been much cheaper and considerably less complex to simply give all of the uninsured Cadillac health plans for life. I am a firm believer that health care reform was and is needed, and I have been advocating for it for several years. It needs to be done correctly, though, and in a way that does not create different levels of access and treatment.

There is no question that the American people are distracted by sports and entertainment and that we confer godlike status on actors and some athletes. There is also no question that we could do more to enhance our knowledge about important issues. However, to assume that the American people are stupid and uncaring and to design programs and speeches around that assumption is arrogant, disrespectful and, frankly, very shortsighted. As has famously been said, "You can fool some of the people all of the time and all of the people some of the time, but you can't fool all of the people all of the time."

This most recent revelation by the unmasking of one of the chief architects of Obamacare is far from the first and only indication of a pattern of deception and manipulation by the current administration. There appears to be overt contempt for the intelligence of the populace by people who would have us believe that the Benghazi disaster was caused by an ill-defined and little-watched video, and that there was not even a smidgen of evidence of wrongdoing surrounding the "phony" Internal Revenue Service scandal, and that the government would never engage in spying on its own citizens without cause. Unfortunately, the administration knows that it can say virtually anything, and that there are some people who are so desperate to believe that it will be accepted as truth. They also know that many members of the mainstream media subscribe to their same ideology and will protect them, regardless of the consequences.

Only people who doubt the analytical ability of the populace would believe that giving people free phones and generous entitlements could purchase their loyalty forever. Only people who think the populace consists of morons would believe that they could keep delaying the employer mandate portion of Obamacare until after an important election, and that people would not realize that they were being manipulated.

The recent election results indicate the resurgence of an informed populace in our nation. Even though the awakening is not complete, I believe Gruber may be proved wrong about the intellect of the American people.

~~~

Illegal Executive Orders Reward Illegal Immigration

November 26, 2014

Like millions of other Americans, I appreciate the plight of billions of people throughout the world who would like nothing more than to find themselves in the United States, where they could enjoy a much higher standard of living and wonderful opportunities for advancement.

It certainly seems like a compassionate thing to offer them legal status in America and the opportunity to pursue their dreams. It should first be considered, however, that we have millions of people already mired in dire poverty in our inner cities, rural townships and places such as Appalachia who would certainly appreciate a helping hand before we extend one to foreigners. The same principle is seen when you board an airplane and hear the announcement, "In case of an emergency, oxygen masks will drop from the ceiling. Put yours on first, and then administer help to those around you." There are many around us already in need of help.

According to President Obama, only those five million or so illegals who have been in America for five years or more will benefit from his largesse. He indicates that they will not be eligible for health care and other benefits. Obviously, this fits right into the same category as his promise: "If you like your doctor, you can keep your doctor."

Once illegals have legal status, it will be difficult to deny them any of the multitudinous entitlements that are freely distributed throughout our society. Also, we must remember that illegals who have been here for less than five years only have to claim that they have been here longer than that in order to collect goodies. In effect, instead of helping five million people, we probably will be aiding at least twice that many.

Even this would not be a problem if we had plenty of money. The sad fact is our national debt is approaching $18 trillion. If you paid that back at a rate of $1 billion per day, it would take nearly 50 years. Many powerful nations before us have met their fate through fiscal irresponsibility. What makes our leaders think we are immune from the destructive forces of a shaky financial foundation?

The founders of our nation feared that the time would arise when an individual or group of individuals in our government would become intoxicated with their power and attempt to impose their will upon the entire society through dictatorial decrees rather than through the legal process established by our Constitution. For this reason, they established three separate but equal branches of government, dividing the powers. This ingenious method of power division worked beautifully until recently, but hopefully, we are about to experience a demonstration of how the separation of powers preserves the integrity of our system. It will require that the legislative and judicial branches of government manifest the necessary courage to stand up for the people they represent.

The American people should not be manipulated into believing that they are heartless simply because they want to preserve the rule of law in our nation and look after their own before they take in others. We also have to consider the millions of people who have immigrated here legally, as well as those who are in the queue. It is incredibly unfair to them to grant amnesty to those who have jumped ahead of them in line illegally. I hope all of our government officials will recall the words of the Pledge of Allegiance, with particular emphasis on the part that says: "with liberty and justice for all."

~~~

The Handiwork of Agitators and Manipulators

December 3, 2014

As a pediatric neurosurgeon, I became more than familiar with situations where parents experience the premature loss of a child. There are few things that can compare to the emotional devastation that accompanies such an event. This makes the varied emotional responses of Michael Brown's family more understandable as the tragic events unfolded in Ferguson, Mo.

What is difficult to understand, though, is the benefit that the Ferguson community derives from burning and looting business establishments in their own neighborhoods, especially when unemployment is already a problem. In the meantime, the outside agitators in many cases are sitting in their hotel rooms sipping wine and watching the carnage on television.

Hopefully, people in communities such as Ferguson, like people all over America, are beginning to awaken and realize that they should be more than pawns in the hands of manipulators who, in reality, could not care less about them.

If the outside agitators and manipulators truly cared about Brown and his family, they would have initiated manifestations of concern long before the political spotlight brought attention and prestige to their cause. They would be outraged about the dozens of young men like Brown who die violent non-police-related deaths in cities throughout America every day. They would be emphasizing education, which is the great divide between the haves and the have-nots in America. A well-educated individual in America today can usually write their own ticket, regardless of ethnicity or financial status at birth.

Perhaps it would be useful to highlight the fact that the average American lives to be about 80 years of age. The first 20 to 25 years are spent either preparing oneself through education or not preparing. If you prepare appropriately, you have 55 to 60 years to reap the benefits. If you fail to prepare, you have 55 to 60 years to suffer the consequences.

This is not to say that every component of our society should not be involved in trying to produce good outcomes for all of our young people. But we need to emphasize that the person who has the most to do with what happens to you in life is you. We must resist the victim mentality that is peddled by so many agitators and manipulators. If you believe you are a victim, you are, and you begin to act like a victim. This renders you an easy target for manipulation -- even the kind that produces completely irrational and self-injurious behavior.

Is there racism and unfairness in our society? Of course there is, and it will persist as long as there are people with small, selfish minds. I believe it would be wise to encourage our people to focus on the numerous opportunities available to them rather than on the bigotry that exists. As a youngster, I grew up with a mother who said, "If you walk into an auditorium full of racist, bigoted people, you don't have a problem; they have a problem. Because they will all cringe and wonder if you're going to sit next to them; whereas you can sit anywhere you want." In other words, don't let your life be ruined by being sucked into the pathological state of someone else.

We have too many important problems to solve in America today to allow ourselves to be consumed by actual or perceived injustices perpetrated by others. We can solve many of those problems by keeping an open mind and considering things from the viewpoints of others. This can lead to constructive conversations about ways to heal the many rifts in our society.

One would have to be blind not to be able to see that we have become more divided on issues of race, gender, age, economic status and religion. What happened in Ferguson is a manifestation of that division. It is not a declaration of what our society has become or a harbinger of our future.

~~~

Democrats' Wasteful Torture Report

December 17, 2014

The recent release of a Senate report commissioned by Democrats regarding torture of terrorism suspects in order to obtain vital information was a waste of $40 million of taxpayer money.

It already had been documented extensively that three suspects were waterboarded and that sleep deprivation and other such techniques were used to extract vital information from terrorists. Though the report says otherwise, that information played a part in the apprehension or annihilation of many upper-echelon terrorist leaders, including Osama bin Laden. The high-profile release of this information at a time when we are engaged in war with various terrorist groups demonstrates a profound lack of wisdom because this information will undoubtedly be used as an effective recruitment tool by our enemies.

Some of the people responsible for the release of this report have publicly acknowledged that it could put members of the military and other Americans at significant risk because they could now become prized targets for revenge. It seems likely that the unwise timing of this information release was politically motivated, seeing as control of the Senate will be in Republican hands in January.

This is a prime example of a potentially lethal disease that has infected Washington, called blind partisanship. It is exhibited when people are more concerned about damaging the other party or enhancing their own party than they are about the welfare of their nation. Of course, we should all be concerned about cruel and unusual treatment of any human being, but we must have enough common sense to recognize that it is foolish to do anything that contributes to the long-term weakening of our military efforts, especially when we are engaged in a war, even though some may not want to call it that.

Unfortunately, conflicts and wars seem to be a part of the human condition from which we cannot escape, even though we must never cease trying. However, when we are involved in a war, we should use every resource available to end it quickly and successfully, including the use of covert weapons and techniques that are not meant for public consumption. It is absolutely foolhardy to believe that everyone is going to abide by the rules of moral war, if there are such things. If we allow our enemies to do anything they want to do, including beheading our citizens, but we feel that we must accord them every courtesy and comfort, our days of winning wars will be over. We should not put our military forces, our intelligence-gathering forces or any of our defensive or offensive personnel in a position of questioning whether we will back them up when a problem arises if they are using their best judgment on behalf of their fellow citizens. This will only cause them to be fearful and tentative at times when definitive and aggressive action is warranted.

The $40 million that was used on this study could have been better employed to study alternative techniques for extracting vital information from unwilling captives, which could be added to our armamentarium. We also need to understand that peace is much more likely to be realized if we are in a position of strength and possess a military force that cannot be challenged. We also might experience more peace if we tried to anticipate and prepare for trouble, as opposed to waiting and simply reacting to ever-increasing problems.

Members of both parties need to take time to figure out who the real enemies are and stop trying to demonize each other. We have a lot to be proud of as Americans. Maybe we should spend time studying and talking about that.

~~~

A Lesson in Optimism from Israel

December 24, 2014

Like many other Americans, I have always had a desire to travel to Israel and visit firsthand the many historical sites of spiritual significance. I was recently afforded the opportunity to fulfill that desire and was not disappointed.

In addition to being greatly inspired, I spoke with numerous Israeli citizens from a variety of backgrounds. One overwhelming theme in those conversations was the feeling of abandonment by the United States government. Some of the more diplomatic individuals said they felt sidelined by a U.S. government that had more important issues to deal with. Of course, they had not forgotten the times that our military and financial aid saved them from utter defeat at the hands of their numerous local enemies.

We must remember that Israel is a small country, about the size of New Jersey, with only 8 million people. It is surrounded by Lebanon, Syria, Jordan, Egypt and the Mediterranean Sea, with several other hostile nations in proximity. Enemy forces are in control of the Gaza Strip and the West Bank, which consists primarily of Samaria and Judea. If not for the Iron Dome missile defense system, the multitudinous rockets launched at Israel this summer from Gaza would have wreaked unimaginable damage on the tiny country. Many Israelis believe, probably correctly, that the aggressiveness of the hostile nations surrounding them is increased when the perception exists that we in the United States are not seriously committed to their protection.

Some will say we have no more of an obligation to Israel than we do to any other country in the Middle East. Perhaps they have forgotten that Israel is one of our staunchest allies and has collaborated with us on many innovative and mutually beneficial products. Having a strong and dependable military ally in what is arguably the most problematic area of the world right now is certainly a tremendous benefit. As a nation, we have a strong Judeo-Christian heritage, which is important to our identity and the strong value system that once characterized our nation. Furthermore, other nations watch how we treat our longtime ally, since that might serve as a harbinger of how we would treat them.

In my many conversations in Israel, the level of optimism I found also impressed me. Despite the fact that Israelis must send their children to school in armored buses and take many other life-changing precautions on a daily basis, most of them did not seem to be bitter, and they were determined not to let terrorists take control of their lives. The opportunity to visit their thriving and innovative technology sector will never be forgotten. While birthrates are declining in America and Europe, the Israeli birthrate, slightly over three children per family, is increasing. Historically, pessimistic people do not tend to have increasing birthrates. If they can be optimistic while facing death, hatred and attempted destruction every single day, is there a lesson there for us?

We live in a country with significant personal freedom, a formidable military, significant levels of common decency and numerous economic opportunities. Additionally, we are on the verge of gaining energy independence, which will positively impact our portfolio of diplomatic options. With the courage and fortitude to take advantage of these and many other benefits, there is no reason that optimism should not reign supreme in America.

~~~

The Wisdom of Peace Through Strength

December 31, 2014

It was extremely encouraging to see the United States and Sony eventually stand up to the cyberbullying of the North Koreans by allowing the movie "The Interview" to be released despite threats of retaliation.

Freedom of speech and freedom of expression are hallmarks of American life, and we must jealously guard these values from both internal and external threats. In fact, all of the freedoms guaranteed to American citizens by our Constitution must be steadfastly preserved, or they will be eroded. Vigilance and courage are necessary every day if we are to remain a free society.

I am proud of the president of the United States for taking a tough stand on this issue, although I am not sure that his promise of proportional retaliation is the correct answer. The response should go far beyond proportionality, and an example should be made of the perpetrators by using a host of available options to inflict punishment not be easily forgotten. If we use proportionality as our standard, future adversaries need only consider certain consequences for encroaching on our rights. If, on the other hand, they realize that they will suffer enormous consequences, I believe their adventurism would be tempered.

I do not advocate becoming a bully on the global stage, but I do believe that strength is a quality that is respected by all cultures, regardless of their ideological bent. I remember how much trouble students in my high school in Detroit caused the weak teachers who had no idea of how to control them. There was one teacher, 5 feet tall, who tolerated no foolishness and even the burly football players feared her. You could hear a pin drop in her room, though the same students produced total chaos in other classrooms. She was extremely nice to me and the other cooperative students and would go out of her way to ensure we received a good education. I think the lesson here is obvious.

There was a time when American citizens were relatively safe, no matter where they traveled in the world. Everyone knew that there would be significant consequences for harming Americans. Today, not only is the fear gone, but there is little respect for our leaders because our nation appears to be a paper tiger. This is a situation that can be quickly rectified with courageous and principled leadership. Many will remember the Iran hostage crisis in the late 1970s and early 1980s. During that time, we had a president who was neither feared nor respected. On the day Ronald Reagan was inaugurated as president, the hostages were released.

It is imperative that, as a nation, we say what we mean and we mean what we say. This contributes to the safety and stability of the world and, in the long run, will cost us less money and fewer lives. Our friends around the world should have no better ally, and our enemies should have no fiercer foe. We certainly do not need to make everyone conform to our values, but we must protect and defend those values, including freedom of expression. We should never yield to evil nor should we ignore it at our own peril.

~~~

Dispelling the Myth of Haves and Have-Nots in America

January 7, 2015

The U.S Constitution was designed to preserve the freedom and rights of all citizens. Our Declaration of Independence states that all men are created equal and that we have certain God-given rights. With documents like these, how have we arrived at the state of such discord between purported haves and have-nots in our society?

Some will try, of course, to discount any discussion of this topic by talking about the treatment of slaves, indentured servants, Native Americans and others who historically were not treated well. I am willing to acknowledge that the same human frailties that characterized societies throughout the world found their way into America, but it is unfair to demonize a nation and its many constituents based on the shortcomings of some of its members. Those who condemn America for its past seldom talk about the tremendous good and generosity that have been demonstrated by the country that cannot be denied the title of most benign pinnacle nation in the history of the world.

One of the reasons that I find the concept of royalty and celebrity amusing is watching people putting on airs and trying to act like someone special when they are acutely aware that, in fact, they are just like everyone else. In my opinion, either everyone is special, or no one is special. America is supposed to be a place of equality, and whether a person is homeless or a billionaire, he should be treated well and equally. There is no social class or political class that has the right to lord it over everyone else unless "we the people" confer such power upon them or allow them to confer it upon themselves without resistance.

Obviously, the billionaire can afford to pay for certain things like luxurious homes and cars and the best seats on airplanes and at the theater. There is nothing wrong with that. It should not cause resentment in a society in which anyone is free to work hard and use their God-given talents to excel and increase their own value in the marketplace. Some will not admit it, but our society would be pretty dreary if everyone shared the same level of poverty with no chance of advancing themselves economically through their own efforts.

I realize that it is not a politically correct thing to say, but the real problem is not the existence of wealthy people among us. Rather, it is the feeling of helplessness and dependency that has been propagated falsely throughout many facets of our society. Perhaps it would be wise for our government to look back at the history of our nation and realize that the unprecedented rise of America to pinnacle status occurred because people knew that if they worked hard and were innovative and productive, they and their families would be the beneficiaries of that labor. I am not saying that taxes should not be paid in a fair manner, but I am saying that the government will never be successful in resolving income disparity and other social problems by taking from the haves and giving to the have-nots.

The great equalizer in America remains education. A good education or the acquisition of technical skills provides tremendous options for everyone, regardless of their birth circumstances. We live in a country where people are free to move without penalty to any state where jobs are available. We need to emphasize the fact that almost any kind of employment confers knowledge and skills that become valuable when trying to move up the economic ladder. One also acquires contacts that can be quite useful for those with knowledge and skill.

Those who have achieved great financial success should be encouraged to invest in their fellow Americans, with the return on investment being the transformation from dependency to proud achiever of the American dream.

~~~

Investing in a Better America: Communities Raise Productive Citizens, Government Leaves Them Dependent

January 15, 2015

Warren Buffett became very rich and famous because he is a terrific investor. Not everyone agrees with his political stances, but his ability to achieve great return on investment is unquestioned.

Most people are familiar with the parable in the Bible of the 10 talents. Two servants who made wise investments were praised and rewarded with even more opportunities, while the one servant who simply attempted to preserve his talent was referred to as wicked, and his one talent was taken from him.

The point is, we have these very complex brains for a reason. Our intricate frontal lobes allow us to extract information from the past and the present, process it and project it into the future as a plan. This means we can plan, strategize and figure out ways to maximize the return on our investment. If we are observant and analytical, we also have the ability to see what is happening in our environment and take steps to change direction if we don't like it, or accelerate down the pathway if we do like what we are seeing.

An examination of American society today would show that we are consolidating power in the hands of relatively few politically powerful or financially powerful individuals, while the middle class, which was once the seat of power, is rapidly shrinking and the dependent class is rapidly expanding. This was clearly not the model the Founders of this nation were trying to create. In fact, our Constitution was designed to prevent this from occurring. Instead of complaining and despairing, we the people must recognize that this nation was built around us and not around the government. The government is supposed to exist for the purpose of facilitating life, liberty and the pursuit of happiness for the citizens of this nation. It must conform to our will, rather than impose its will upon us.

When it comes to investing in the future of our country, we should remember that we had a meteoric rise among the nations of the world because we quickly developed a "can-do attitude." Investments that return us to that kind of thinking will be extremely valuable. Instead of fighting each other, we should use our collective intellect to fashion programs that allow us to invest in our fellow Americans, with the return on investment being deliverance from a state of dependency and realization of the tremendous potential for achievement that resides in each of us -- regardless of station of birth. We can indeed become successful investors.

I'm not saying the government is wicked, but like the wicked servant, its programs confine people to a state of dependency rather than advancing them and empowering them to become independent contributors to society.

A tremendous amount of resources resides in American business, industry, Wall Street, churches, charitable community organizations and private families. I have witnessed a number of impressive organizations around the country whose members have decided without government intervention to invest in less fortunate members of their own communities with spectacular results.

Every person we in the private sector invest in is likely to become a contributor to society, which ultimately helps to raise the tide that floats all boats. The purveyors of hatred and division don't like our system and believe we should all worship at the throne of government. They wish to create dissatisfaction with the current system in order to fertilize the ground for a fundamental change.

We don't need a change. We need a fix. With the can-do attitude that was once such an important part of our identity, we can achieve the greatest return on investment our nation has ever seen.

~~~

Choosing the Challenging Road to Reconciliation

January 21, 2015

A few days ago, I had the pleasure of sitting down with Edward Mullins, president of the Sergeants Benevolent Association of the New York Police Department, to discuss potential ways to improve community-police relationships. He has been working with outstanding community leaders such as Pastor A.R. Bernard, and they sincerely want to achieve a highly successful outcome to a problem of trust that has spread throughout the nation.

One of their proposals involves the establishment of police-sponsored athletic leagues throughout the city. There would be friendly competition between the teams, which would be composed of community residents and police. This would, of course, allow both sides to get a chance to know each other and form a relationship that is not adversarial.

Most of human societal progress is accomplished through relationships. People who are traditional adversaries can rapidly become friends when they work together, get to know each other and develop positive relationships. This opens the doors to communication, and people tend to give each other the benefit of the doubt when they know them. On the other hand, when communication breaks down, as it frequently does before divorce, the two previously friendly partners often become bitter enemies.

I have no doubt that solutions like this one and others proposed by Mullins would be very helpful not only in New York City, but also across the nation. Unfortunately, there are those in our society who will continue to endeavor to stir up strife and fuel hatred. These individuals wish to create dissatisfaction in almost all areas of American life. Thus, we have a war on women, age wars, income wars, race wars and religious wars. If it appears that our society is falling apart at the seams, it creates more fertile ground for a fundamental change. This divide-and-conquer strategy has proved effective for many groups wishing to topple a prevailing culture over the years. It also will be effective in creating chaos and anarchy in our society if we do not begin to more carefully analyze and control our emotional reactions.

If, like Mullins and Bernard, we are willing to sit down and rationally discuss solutions to our differences, we can build a bond of unity that would be stronger than the inevitable conflicts that accompany life in a complex society. Yes, it does require conviction, effort and even some humility to be willing to make oneself vulnerable enough to invest in a relationship with someone previously unknown. The alternative of continued and worsening hatred and violence makes such a risk extremely worthwhile for all parties involved.

We the American people are not enemies, and we certainly do not need to continue to try to tear one another down, especially when groups like the Islamic State are trying to destroy us. Our fractured relationships simply make their job easier. We must be able to look ahead and see the big picture of strength that results from a united front and peace that is derived through cultivating friendships.

~~~

When Politics Defy Reality: The Real State of the Union Features Dishonesty and Deception

January 28, 2015

In his recent State of the Union address, President Obama was upbeat and inspiring, particularly if a listener had no prior knowledge of his many speeches that were quite similar but bore no fruit. It almost appeared that he was living in an alternate universe that bore no resemblance to present-day America and the current global stage.

He boasted that the economy was doing very well and that unemployment had been cut in half since he took office. Perhaps someone should educate him about the labor force participation rate, which is at its lowest point in the past 36 years and reflects the number of people who are actually working versus the number of people who are eligible to work. The unemployment rate can easily be manipulated in whichever direction one desires by including and excluding certain groups of people.

He also boasted about the record-high stock market numbers. He failed to indicate that savings accounts and certain types of bonds, which used to be the mechanism whereby average Americans could enhance their net worth over a long period of time, were no longer appealing, and that the stock market was one of the few places where gains could be made. While the stock market has always been particularly relevant to the wealthier members of society, the influx of these smaller investors is further driving the income gap.

He talked about the need to further tax the rich because they are not paying their fair share. He failed to mention that the top 1 percent pays 37 percent of the federal income taxes, while earning 19 percent of the income. Since he is so concerned about fairness, perhaps he should consider a proportional (flat) tax, which hits everyone according to their ability to pay. To make this even more fair, we could eliminate all loopholes.

155

His claim that we are winning the war against terrorism, even though he failed to mention the name of the radical Islamists who are behind the terror, was almost laughable in light of its rapid growth and spread throughout the world. He appeared not to recognize that our premature withdrawal of troops from Iraq was a mistake that facilitated the development of the Islamic State. His bravado about chasing the terrorists and eliminating them bears no resemblance to his actual policies and demonstrates his contempt for the intelligence of his audience.

He demonstrated great courage in talking about how the Affordable Care Act is actually resulting in a reduction in health care spending. This may be true on some levels, but the reason for that decreased spending is secondary to the reluctance of people to seek medical care when they have deductibles of thousands of dollars.

I wonder whether he and his team ever considered the fact that we spend $400 billion a year on Medicaid, which covers about 80 million Americans. That's about $5,000 per enrollee. Many of the concierge practices that target those who are financially well off only cost $2,000 to $3,000 per year. If we spent Medicaid dollars wisely, we could provide excellent care, including catastrophic care, for considerably less money than we are spending now.

The president also made some fantastic comments that served as applause lines regarding energy, education and a few other subjects. The real state of the union is characterized by dishonesty and deception. Instead of pretending that everything is rosy, perhaps it would be wise for the president to replay the part of the speech about bipartisan cooperation and then figure out how his multiple veto threats, failure to communicate and reluctance to seek bipartisan solutions fit the theme of his address.

~~~

Vaccinations Are for the Good of the Nation

February 11, 2015

There has been much debate recently over vaccination mandates, particularly in response to the measles outbreak currently taking place throughout the country.

At this juncture, there have been 102 confirmed measles cases in the U.S. during 2015, with 59 of them linked to a December 2014 visit to the Disneyland theme park in Southern California. (It is important to note that 11 of the cases associated with Disneyland were detected last year and, consequently, fall within the 2014 measles count.) This large outbreak has spread to at least a half-dozen other states, and the Centers for Disease Control and Prevention is currently requesting that all health care professionals "consider measles when evaluating patients with febrile rash and ask about a patient's vaccine status, recent travel history and contact with individuals who have febrile rash illness."

One must understand that there is no specific antiviral therapy for measles and that 90 percent of those who are not vaccinated will contract measles if they are indeed exposed to the virus. This explains why Arizona health officials are monitoring more than 1,000 people after potential exposure to measles. These are pretty staggering numbers that should concern not only parents and children, but also the general populace.

I have been asked many times throughout the past week for my thoughts concerning the issue of vaccines. The important thing is to make sure the public understands that there is no substantial risk from vaccines and that the benefits are very significant. Although I strongly believe in individual rights and the rights of parents to raise their children as they see fit, I also recognize that public health and public safety are extremely important in our society. Certain communicable diseases have been largely eradicated by immunization policies in this country. We should not allow those diseases to return by forgoing safety immunization programs for philosophical, religious or other reasons when we have the means to eradicate them.

Obviously, there are exceptional situations to virtually everything, and we must have a mechanism whereby those can be heard. Nevertheless, there is public policy and health policy that we have to pay attention to regarding this matter. We already have policies in place at schools that require immunization records -- this is a positive thing. Studies have shown over the course of time that the risk-benefit ratio for vaccination is grossly in favor of being vaccinated as opposed to not.

There is no question that immunizations have been effective in eliminating diseases such as smallpox, which was devastating and lethal. When you have diseases that have been demonstrably curtailed or eradicated by immunization, why would you even think about not doing it? Certain people have discussed the possibility of potential health risks from vaccinations. I am not aware of scientific evidence of a direct correlation. I think there probably are people who may make a correlation where one does not exist, and that fear subsequently ignites, catches fire and spreads. But it is important to educate the public about what evidence actually exists.

I am very much in favor of parental rights for certain types of things. I am in favor of you and I having the freedom to drive a car. But do we have a right to drive without wearing our seatbelts? Do we have a right to text while we are driving? Studies have demonstrated that those are dangerous things to do, so it becomes a public safety issue. You have to be able to distinguish our rights versus the rights of the society in which we live, because we are all in this thing together. We have to be cognizant of the other people around us, and we must always bear in mind the safety of the population. That is key, and that is one of the responsibilities of government.

I am a small-government person, and I greatly oppose government intrusion into everything. Still, it is essential that we distinguish between those things that are important and those things that are just intruding upon our basic privacy. Whether to participate in childhood immunizations would be an individual choice if individuals were the only ones affected, but as previously mentioned, our children are part of our larger community. None of us lives in isolation. Your decision does not affect only you -- it also affects your fellow Americans.

~~~

We Have Met the Enemy, and He Is Not Us

February 18, 2015

The graphic pictures of a Jordanian pilot being burned alive by militants from the Islamic State, or ISIS, were chilling and raised doubts about the humanity of the Islamic terrorists capable of such barbarism. This coupled with beheadings and crucifixions gives us a better understanding of the evil we, along with the rest of the world, are facing.

These terrorists have stated their intention to annihilate Israel and to destroy the American way of life, which they consider corrupt and evil. Undoubtedly, we in America have our faults like every other country inhabited by human beings, but it requires the suspension of knowledge of accurate American history to believe, as some do, that we are the source of much of the trouble in the world. Conditions in the world have improved more dramatically since the advent of the United States than at any other time in human history. Our innovation and compassion have provided one of the highest standards of living in the world while lifting conditions in many other nations.

Understanding that we are not evil makes it easier to identify evil elsewhere and to combat it effectively. When we accept the falsehood that everyone is equally bad, and, therefore, we have no right or obligation to interfere with atrocities occurring elsewhere in the world, we facilitate the development and growth of groups such as ISIS, which are not dissimilar to the adherents of Adolf Hitler, who also aspired to world domination. An objective analysis of American history will demonstrate that we were late in joining the efforts of others to combat evil during both World War I and World War II. Hopefully, we have learned from these mistakes that it is better to fight enemies while they are in their adolescent stages than to wait until they have fully matured and pose a much greater threat.

I certainly do not believe that we need to involve ourselves in every conflict on the planet, and I believe we involved ourselves in the Vietnam conflict without clear goals or strategies. Hopefully, we learned from that experience that it is neither wise nor correct to try to impose our way of life on others. I also believe that there were better ways to handle Saddam Hussein than a full-fledged military confrontation. Those better ways would have involved a plan for Iraqi leadership over the long term. These unfortunate experiences have made some gun-shy to the point that they probably would rather be invaded than adopt an offensive war posture.

This is a critical time in the history of the world, and we must clear our heads and think logically about the consequences of underestimating the threat posed by a host of Islamic terrorist groups. It is clear that they have a plan that they believe will yield a victory in their quest for world domination. Some in our country are arrogant enough to believe such a goal is preposterous. Others believe our time has come and gone and resistance is useless.

Both of these beliefs are absolutely wrong and do not take into account the strength and resolve inherent in the American character. The battle we are entering will be difficult and fraught with surprises, but as Winston Churchill said, "You ask, what is our aim? I can answer in one word. It is victory. Victory at all costs. Victory in spite of all terrors. Victory, however long and hard the road may be, for without victory, there is no survival."

~~~

Applauding an Elegant Conservative

February 25, 2015

Recently, I was temporarily placed on the Southern Poverty Law Center's watch list for extremism simply because I vocally support traditional marriage. I remember thinking: When did advocating for lifelong love between one man and one woman become a hate crime? Fortunately, the group saw the folly of its ways and apologized, removing me from the list.

It was a small battle, a blip in the daily life of someone who has entered the political arena. And I enjoyed the support of many who rallied in the conservative media to my cause to help reverse such a silly distinction. But it wasn't that long ago when liberal extremism tried to suffocate traditional values, and there were few media voices to come to the rescue.

There was one, though, so powerful and elegant, persistent yet graceful. Her name is Phyllis Schlafly. And for the past 90 years she has been a tireless advocate for the nuclear family, for traditional marriage and for common-sense conservatism that resists injecting government into every aspect of our lives. On Wednesday night, she will be honored at the Paul Weyrich Awards dinner that precedes the start of the annual Conservative Political Action Conference.

Schlafly fought battles most lacked the courage to fight, and time and again she won. She has been credited for single-handedly stopping the Equal Rights Amendment, which in the 1970s was racing on a media freight train toward ratification. Schlafly stopped it dead in its tracks. It was not because she didn't believe women deserve rights, but rather because she rightfully recognized the ERA was skewed toward favoring young professional women, and that it would punish middle-aged and older women who chose to stay at home and raise their families by taking away "dependent wife" benefits under Social Security and alimony.

In those days, it took courage and lots of hard work to roll back what a liberal media had started in motion. But Schlafly succeeded because she was intellectually honest, impassioned and skilled in not only communicating the fight, but also in waging it. Likewise, she has relentlessly fought for life, recognizing early on that the Roe v. Wade decision would be one of the Supreme Court's worst decisions.

Through good and bad economic times, and the ebb and flow of conservative activism, Phyllis Schlafly has remained a steady voice for common sense and traditional values. Her speeches, books, TV appearances and radio commentaries blazed the way for modern conservatism while also protecting the rights of traditional families from the onslaught of Hollywood's culture wars.

Her voice is as relevant and strong today as it was more than a half-century ago when she made the famous case for Barry Goldwater's conservatism in her great book "A Choice, Not An Echo." In her 2014 book "Who Killed the American Family?" she eloquently touched my heart with her keen insights on how President Obama's agenda and decades of prior liberal tax-code changes and court interference have substituted government intervention for parenting and federal dependency for self-reliance.

Like she has for most of 90 years on this planet, Schlafly cut right to the chase in diagnosing the problem with America today. In plain, simple and compelling language, she rightfully declared that "the government is making ordinary decisions about what the kid does that ought to be made by the mothers and fathers." So simple a declaration, and yet so true.

For those who believe this battle is already lost or isn't worth fighting anymore because the cards are stacked against conservatives, I implore you to step back and examine the extraordinary life of Phyllis Schlafly. She has proved that what seemed impossible can be achieved. She has lived a life of virtue and has never been tempted to compromise. And she has made the most compelling case that the family unit must be preserved in order for America's greatness to extend into future generations. For that extraordinary contribution, I salute her on this special day.

~~~

A Leader and a Speech We Can All Appreciate

March 11, 2015

Israeli Prime Minister Benjamin Netanyahu showed great leadership when delivering his speech to a joint session of Congress regarding America's potential nuclear deal with Iran. History and our past relations with Netanyahu indicate that the prime minister has earned some trust, and no matter what side of the aisle we stand on, we must stand with Israel.

Last December, I had the magnificent opportunity to travel to Israel and visit many historical sites of spiritual importance. After speaking with many Israeli citizens and witnessing firsthand the beauty of a nation with so much pride, I could not help but think of how we as the United States have a strong Judeo-Christian heritage. Israel is one of our strongest allies, and acknowledging the history that we share is important to our identity and to the promising value system we maintain.

The country of Iran continues to conceal aspects of its nuclear program, and thus its compliance is heavily questioned. Iran's regime and its quest for nuclear weapons is not merely a Jewish problem, but rather it poses a substantial and realistic threat to world peace. As was expressed by Netanyahu, things undoubtedly will become worse if there is a deal that gives the Iranians protection and enables them to continue flagrantly operating secret nuclear facilities (as they had been doing in Natanz and Qom) while ostensibly invested in a diplomatic process with the United States.

We must not allow them to continue to enrich uranium and maintain their enormous nuclear infrastructure. According to estimates, Iran could have 190,000 centrifuges enriching uranium within a matter of weeks. A "breakout time" to a nuclear bomb ("breakout time" referring to the amount of time it takes to accumulate enough weapons-grade uranium or plutonium for a nuclear bomb) would be approximately one year, according to U.S. assessment. In February of 2014, the Institute for Science and International Security estimated this time period to stand at roughly two months.

Meanwhile, the IAEA (or the International Atomic Energy Agency, which is the United Nations' nuclear watchdog agency) continues to report that Iran refuses to be transparent with IAEA inspectors about its military nuclear program. The current deal with Iran allows for various concessions, including the inability to destroy any nuclear facilities, as well as enabling all restrictions on Iran's nuclear program to automatically expire in a decade. Does that sound comforting to you?

As the United States works to prevent Iran from acquiring a nuclear weapon, we are also dealing with ISIS as a formidable enemy that threatens our way of life. Every resource available should be used to eradicate the threat of ISIS while it is still in its adolescent stage. That means using every military apparatus we have: banking facilities, sanctions, you name it. And I would not hesitate to put boots on the ground, because nothing should be off the table.

This whole concept of "no boots on the ground because of what happened in Iraq" is silly. The threat that Saddam Hussein and al-Qaida posed at that time was on a completely different level from what we are looking at now. It is immature to equate the two in terms of reactions. ISIS wants to destroy our way of life and us. We have two choices: We can sit back and wait for them, or we can use the resources we have to destroy them.

We need to be the leader and take serious action. I am extraordinarily concerned about the fact that we are not responding to the barbaric acts that are taking place, as there is a tremendous leadership void. A coalition will form if it has a leader.

I would commit everything to eliminating ISIS right now. We have to make sure that our military, which is extremely talented and maintains very good leadership, is not put into a compromised position where we are trying to micromanage things. Otherwise, we will be exposing many people to a state of grave danger.

Across the globe, citizens are dealing with an evil in today's society that is threatening Christians, Jews and anyone who does not believe as ISIS does. If we allow it to continue to grow, it will become a big tree with lots of branches and roots, rather than the bush it is now. The lack of an adequate response to both ISIS and Iran will endanger not only us in the long run, but the entire world.

~~~

The Mighty Internet

March 18, 2015

There is one place to go where you can find out anything about anyone and any moment in history. That place is called the Internet, and yes, you are using it to read this article.

A few decades ago, it would have been considered a luxury, but now it is truly a fixture of life. We seemingly would not be able to live without it -- despite the fact that the world did indeed operate without the Internet before its creation. This global system of interconnected computer networks that links billions of devices worldwide has changed the way we live our lives, for both the good and the bad. As millions of academic, business, social, government, private and public networks come together to provide and receive information, I find it rather remarkable how far we have come in the world of technology. Bravo to those who have helped us reach this place.

I think it is worth discussing the issue of the new net neutrality rules concerning the Internet. When the Federal Communications Commission (FCC) voted to implement the new rules, which make Internet service providers treat all legal content equally, I immediately shuddered at the thought of more government control in our lives.

Essentially, the government is going to regulate the Internet as a public utility so that content providers (such as Amazon and Netflix) cannot pay Internet service providers (like Comcast and Verizon) to deliver their content faster than others -- hence the term "fast lanes."

It is imperative that the government administer antitrust laws and safeguard consumers' ability to choose systems and Internet providers. But to restrict people from paying for something better or faster is not a sound idea. The Internet still has enormous room for growth and innovation, and net neutrality has the potential to suppress said innovation, as business models and novel approaches are hampered by governmental regulation.

With so much potential for future Internet advancements, I frequently have been asked: "What is the impact of technology on our lives, and what are some issues surrounding it?" There obviously is a plethora of positive attributes associated with the Internet and what it enables us to do on a daily basis. We see the Internet utilized in law enforcement to aid our officers, as well as in our classrooms to educate our youth. But this truth-telling machine of the Internet -- what does it say about us as a world? Can it tell us why a war is imminent? Can it reveal our secrets and our leaders? Can we trust the Internet to be all things for us -- the identifier of our enemies and friends, of whom we should date and even marry?

I am raising these questions to spark self-reflection and consideration of the ways in which the Internet affects your life and the role it plays.

It is fitting that Facebook updated its community guidelines this past week in order to be more transparent regarding what the social network deems appropriate content for display. While the company claims its rules and standards remain the same, the network evidently felt obligated to make its stance on various issues clearer for users. Facebook says the standards are crafted to "create an environment where people feel motivated to treat each other with empathy and respect." The updated community standards page clarifies for Facebook's billion-plus users what the network considers safe practices and proper etiquette regarding respect for fellow users and how it handles the security of your account and the protection of your intellectual property.

Standards like these really should be adopted by all people who use the Internet, whether or not they use Facebook. While I am a big proponent of freedom of speech, I believe there is no place for attacks based on race, ethnicity, religion, gender or sexual orientation. Also, we should be very careful about the personal information we post online. Never give up too much of your life via photographs and financial data, because the Internet is a large place, and not everyone utilizing it has the best intentions.

The key is to know how to use the Internet without it using you. Otherwise, you could be subject to unfortunate situations.

~~~

Education: The Future Depends on It

April 1, 2015

Over the past few months in cities throughout the country, we have seen harsh moments that have been characterized as "racial incidents." Whether it be Ferguson, Mo., New York City or Los Angeles, these events continue to occur in states regardless of which party dominates the political landscape.

The three cities previously mentioned are considered Democratic strongholds, which shows us that this is a problem regardless of who is in charge. But what exactly is the problem? What are we missing, or is there something that we are not talking about enough? Can we say it is just one thing that can be summed up as police brutality?

I think it would be ignorant to say there is just one thing that leads to situations like these. There are many things that we need to improve on as a nation. Better training for law enforcement is undoubtedly one of them. Police body cameras to record incidents would be a step in the right direction.

There is also a dire need to devote substantial energy to what is going on in cities like Chicago, Detroit, New Orleans and Washington, D.C., where we witness a plethora of violence, shootings and murder all the time. Teenage pregnancy is all too prevalent in these areas, as well. As women give birth at a young age, it hinders their ability to continue their education due to the significant responsibility of caring for a child. Without the education required for jobs with reasonable wages, the children are eventually forced into poverty, and the cycle of dependence continues. I have said it before: We should focus on child-care facilities that would allow unwed mothers to get their general education development or higher degree and become self-supporting.

Yes, education is the great divide in our country. A well-educated individual in America can usually write their own ticket in today's world, regardless of ethnicity, race, gender or financial status at birth. My whole medical career as a pediatric neurosurgeon was focused on young people and enhancing their lives. We would do everything we possibly could to not only give children longevity, but also quality of life.

Now that I've retired from medicine, I am just as interested in the quality of their future. That is why it is so important to emphasize education. It also is very important for us to emphasize fiscal responsibility. Those of us who are adults today are in charge of the finances of tomorrow. Running up huge bills for our children to pay is being fiscally irresponsible.

Common Core has been a hot topic regarding education, and while I think it is important to have standards, putting such a task in the hands of the federal government is naive, as opposed to the sound idea of placing the onus on local municipalities, schools, teachers and parents. The ability to maintain high academic expectations of our students is dependent upon the curriculum and lessons presented in the classroom. While proponents of Common Core may see benefits to such a system, how can the initiative be effective if it imposes confusing experimental teaching methods that our teachers cannot adequately adopt and our parents cannot actively support? Children thrive on confidence and encouragement, neither of which exists in an environment where the education purveyors are uncomfortable with the standards by which they and their pupils are judged.

America, like the rest of the world, is in the process of changing. It can be a good change, or it can be a bad change. I think the way to ensure it is a really good change is to have a lot of our incredibly bright, talented young people involved in the political process early on -- and this can only happen through a great education.

This nation's founders were extremely well educated, and they acknowledged that our system of governance relies upon an informed populace. We need the intellect, savvy and innovative spirit of our children. They should not be outsiders looking in. They should be participants in all aspects of shaping the future of our country, because they are, indeed, the future of our country.

~~~

Financial Literacy

April 8, 2015

When I was a young boy, I was not familiar with the concepts of financial literacy and responsibility. I did understand that luxury and a comfortable lifestyle -- two things I had no experience with -- would only be obtained by making myself valuable to society. After many difficulties in early childhood, I realized that the person who had the most to do with what happened to me in life was me.

Now, as we sit here with formidable annual budget deficits and growing national debt, it is clear that the people who should be the most concerned about our future obligations are the young members of our society who will be saddled with massive taxes if we do not change our ways.

During my college days, students were much more involved in what was going on in the country, and there were frequent marches and protests. Outside of the misguided Occupy Wall Street movement, there has not been much heard from the younger generations about current financial issues. It is essential for the next generation of young people to be exposed to and have a greater interest in what is occurring in our country and throughout the world, because it will profoundly affect their future. Our children and young adults should make their voices heard in order to create some guilt among the people of my generation who are voraciously spending the nation's future resources.

An interest and assiduousness regarding the economy can be instilled through early teaching and exposure to the ideas I alluded to earlier: financial literacy and responsibility. Becoming an informed citizen when it comes to finance certainly makes you a wiser voter and can enhance all of life's experiences, from planning a career to raising a family. Knowledge of basic household economics is critical for all Americans, and preparing our youth with a financial skill set will enable them to plan for a prosperous future. Key principles like balancing a checkbook and knowing that you do not buy a house that costs more than two-and-a-half times your annual income could have saved many Americans from a mountain of adversity prior to the housing crisis.

So what are some steps we can take to steer people in the right direction? On Jan. 29, 2010, President Barack Obama signed an executive order that created the President's Advisory Council on Financial Capability in order to help Americans in understanding financial matters. This council -- which comprises non-governmental representatives with finance-related experience, including financial services, consumer protection and financial access -- was also created to help people make informed financial choices in order to foster financial stability.

On March 31, 2011, Obama said, "As we recover from the worst economic crisis in generations, it is more important than ever to be knowledgeable about the consequences of our financial decisions. ... We recommit to improving financial literacy and ensuring all Americans have access to trustworthy financial services and products."

I agree with the president, as we must integrate important components of personal finance into K-12 education. We also must encourage parents to educate their children in the lifelong pursuit of financial education. The best way to encourage our nation's parents is to provide them with the adequate tools and resources to understand and introduce financial literacy in their homes. With the widespread and ever-growing accumulation of student loan debt in the United States, this is a truly pivotal moment in time.

While balancing a checkbook, thinking through how credit works and understanding how debt accumulates may all seem elementary in nature to some people, there is a surprising number of adult Americans who lack the requisite familiarity. A worthy action step we all could take to help combat financial ignorance includes discussing financial responsibility with a young person in your sphere of influence this month. Help people to understand the incredible potential they have, and help them realize they don't really have to depend on a lot of other people once they are equipped with the proper skills

And when you engage in your next financial endeavor, ask yourself: How will this affect the next generation? You may just realize that the effect is greater than you previously imagined.

~~~

A Time for National Action

April 15, 2015

Last week, I had the pleasure of speaking at the National Action Network's (NAN) 17th annual national convention in New York City. NAN is one of the leading civil rights organizations in the United States. It was founded in 1991 by the Rev. Al Sharpton to "promote a modern civil rights agenda that includes the fight for one standard of justice, decency and equal opportunities for all people regardless of race, religion, nationality or gender."

The convention proved to be a great stage for productive dialogue and conversation through various panels. Some of the topics discussed included housing, health care, law enforcement, corporate finance and education. I voiced my opinion on several of these issues, while also promoting the idea that the choices we make in this world have the most to do with our outcomes. Personal responsibility and self-determination -- not the household into which you are born, the police force in your neighborhood or the color of your skin -- are the key contributing factors of your life.

Sharpton and I have the same goal: to build a brighter, stronger America that provides equal opportunities and access to the underserved and forgotten. However, we have a fundamental difference of opinion regarding the best way to achieve such an end.

I know from my own experience of having been raised in dire poverty by a single mother that education has the power to bridge socio-economic divides and lift entire families out of destitution. My mother, who is the hero in my life, refused to embrace a victim mentality that many do in today's world. That is why I stress the importance of instilling in our children the mindset that they can accomplish anything if they do not think they are victims.

Fifty years ago, this nation began a war on poverty that we have not come close to winning. This is due to the fact that rather than creating a system that lifts people out of a meager financial situation, we have developed a system that perpetuates generational dependence and an inability to escape hardship. The programs established throughout the years have not worked, because the implementation and follow-up procedures do not match the rhetoric heard in press conferences and announcements.

Some have attempted to win the war on poverty and improve the members of our community by holding boycotts and assembling demonstrations. This method has made some people wealthy (the organizers), but not the people it claims to help. It is crucial that through various policies and self-reflection, we get more people from a state of dependence to one of independence. In the African-American community, we do not need to wait for others to help us. We need to use our God-given talents to achieve greatness and lift others up.

Ever since I was introduced into medicine and surgery during my young adulthood, I've seen a plethora of young families in stress, and that has shaped who I am today. As people of all different colors have put their health in my hands, I truly have been able to understand all their brains, brilliance and decency.

I come from dire poverty, not knowing where the next meal would come from. Despite my pedigree as a pediatric neurosurgeon, I have been assumed to be an orderly in the hospital because of my race. I have been through tough times and struggles and can relate to the plight of many.

But our diversity is a blessing, and God has given us all the tools to overcome tribulations and be as productive as the next person. There is no stone we cannot overturn. America achieved prominence in record time because of its talented and diverse population, and the future should be no different. Let us not play into the game of having enemies. Let us come together to hold fast to those principles and family values that got us through troubling times so that we can uplift all communities and foster equality.

~~~

America Needs Clarity and Conviction of Purpose in the Middle East

April 22, 2015

For much of the past century, America has embodied, both in word and in deed, a commitment to freedom and democracy that has improved the lives of billions of people all over the world.

Leaders such as Dwight Eisenhower and Ronald Reagan saw the importance of a foreign policy based on American values and grounded in American leadership. They understood that smart, strategic engagement was the only way to ensure our security, champion our values and advance our interests.

One of the most unstable and dangerous areas of the world today is the Middle East. Events that take place there have serious repercussions all across the globe that directly impact America's national security.

In the Middle East, the United States must return to a position of global leadership -- mere engagement is not enough. And while multilateral diplomacy is important, it, too, is insufficient. The next American president must demonstrate principled leadership that truly reflects our values and protects our interests by demonstrating the strength and resolve necessary to ensure our security.

Rogue regimes and their terrorist allies, sensing an opportunity, are expanding their influence in the Middle East. America's allies are deeply unsettled, worried that the enemies who provide a clear and present danger to them and to us believe that America is either unable or unwilling to counter their advances.

We should not shy away from the responsibility that comes from being the world's lone superpower, nor should we subvert our own unique standing by stooping to embrace regimes opposed to our values that routinely express their hatred for us and sponsor terrorist attacks against our citizens. We must reverse the current course of our nation's policy in the Middle East by clearly demonstrating that we know where America stands and are unafraid to do what is required to protect our interests, our allies and ourselves.

Iran's pursuit of nuclear weapons and hegemony in the Middle East threatens the already tenuous stability throughout the entire region. ISIS terrorists corrupt religion to justify murder, recruiting Western citizens to join in their jihad. A tyrannical regime clings to power in Syria, slaughtering tens of thousands of innocent civilians. Our closest ally in the Middle East, Israel, faces threats from all sides.

Many of these challenges are extremely complex, and America cannot and should not confront all of them alone. But the path forward should involve leading from the front, rallying our allies behind our just cause.

We need to show that our commitment to our friends is more than mere lip service. We must be unyielding in our support of our true allies, never letting trivial or petty disagreements supersede important relationships built over decades. This only serves to undermine our interests and empower our enemies. Our allies across the Middle East must know that the United States will help them in times of crisis and will work closely with them to ensure they remain safe, secure and prosperous.

Moving forward, the world should know where the United States stands. We cannot allow Iran to achieve nuclear-weapons capability. We must ensure that Israel continues to exist as a safe, secure democracy. And we must prevent radical Islam, which celebrates death and seeks to destroy modern society, from achieving a lasting foothold in the region.

When the United States draws red lines and issues ultimatums, we must be prepared to enforce them. Our failure to do so creates the perception that we are weak and uncertain; it emboldens and motivates our enemies. Failure to follow through on our promises creates the perception that we are a paper tiger, and it inspires radical regimes and terrorist groups to increase their aggressive pursuits that run counter to our own hopes for the region.

The global community, and especially those regimes whose nefarious actions should exclude them from the family of nations, must understand that the United States means what it says. Though we should always exhaust diplomatic options first, we must also be unafraid to confront aggression in kind and never feel forced to apologize for doing what we must to defend our nation and the security of our citizens.

With an overarching philosophy based on our values, we should champion policies that support our interests: security, stability and economic opportunity. Historically, we have engaged other nations in pursuit of these interests, and ensuring that our future remains bright requires continued work in these areas. Clearly articulating our foreign-policy vision in the Middle East will provide comfort to our friends, and it also will provide clarity -- and serve as a warning and a deterrent -- to those who wish us harm.

Terrorists, rogue states and nations with hostile agendas running counter to our own must understand that America not only takes notice of their actions, but we will punish such behaviors, and never abide or reward them.

In his first inaugural address, President Eisenhower said, "Forces of good and evil are massed and armed and opposed as rarely before in history. Freedom is pitted against slavery, lightness against dark." Eisenhower was referring to communism, of course, but his words ring true for today's Middle East, as well.

In order to ensure the safety, security and prosperity of our great country, we must clearly define our goals in the Middle East. America must support our friends in every way possible and work hard to prevent our enemies from harming our interests. We must reignite American leadership to stabilize the Middle East, protect our allies, and defend our nation, our allies and our interests.

The United States must return a sense of moral clarity and conviction of purpose to our Middle East policy, and we must be willing to lead in a manner that reflects our values.

~~~

My Voting Evolution

April 29, 2015

I grew up in Detroit, in an environment where one was supposed to be Democrat and where people constantly told me that Republicans were evil and racist people. As I entered my teenage years, I did not have the exposure to the political world that is more easily afforded young people via technology today. I did not develop my own train of thought regarding political parties and what politicians could help accomplish for myself, my family and my community.

The first presidential election in which I could vote was in 1972, which saw George McGovern face off against Richard Nixon. As a student of Yale University, I found it comforting to follow my classmates and vote Democrat. While McGovern fell dramatically to Nixon, I still identified with Democrats and voted for Jimmy Carter in 1976 as he battled Gerald Ford. I decided to vote for Carter again in 1980, as he seemed like a decent person. However, he would lose in a landslide to Ronald Reagan.

During Reagan's first term, I had just begun my neurosurgery residency at the Johns Hopkins Hospital in Baltimore. I had exposure to many patients with unfulfilled lives because they were becoming dependent on government programs, and it struck me as the wrong way to go. Almost all of my patients were on some kind of medical assistance and social welfare programs, and their lives were in shambles.

Simultaneously, I listened to President Reagan's speeches and he did not seem evil and racist, as portrayed by the Democrats. In fact, I viewed him as a decent, trustworthy man who was a true leader. Thus, in 1984, I voted for Reagan. This was a pivotal moment in my life, as I allowed myself to make a decision based on who the candidate was and his capabilities. This was contrary to voting based solely on party affiliation, which I had been conditioned to do my entire young adulthood.

Fast forward to 1988 and 1992. I voted for George H.W. Bush, who seemed very pro-American and preached the importance of caring for everyone. My ways of voting Republican continued in 1996 because of Bob Dole's strong military and war record (U.S. Army second lieutenant during World War II), a man who appeared compassionate, was a strong leader, and who thrived as Senate majority leader for eight years. Although Dole did not win, I still believed strongly in my conservative values and realized that the more you build in your life and in your career, and the more you raise children, the more conservative and the less liberal you become.

When George W. Bush campaigned in 2000, his policies and general philosophy appeared more in line with my beliefs. The same held true in 2004, and I was intent on him seeing through what he had started in Iraq and other parts of the world. The country had been exposed to dangerous forces that threatened our way of life, and President Bush was adamant about protecting our nation.

2008 was monumental for the United States, with Barack Obama becoming the first African-American with a legitimate chance of winning the presidency. I was torn by history, being an African-American myself and understanding the tribulations that my race had endured over time. Nevertheless, I understood that Obama did not represent me as an American. Instead, Senator John McCain's principles and military experience earned him my vote.

The financial crisis that devastated our economy would prove to be an important factor in the next election, and I believed we needed someone with sound business acumen and an ability to lead the nation towards prosperity. With the risk of a growing national debt and frivolous spending, it was clear to me that the man I voted for, Mitt Romney, would be a more able candidate in uplifting the economy. Voting is critical to holding our elected officials accountable for their actions and inactions. Continue to exercise that amazing privilege and vote the leadership that is necessary to move our great nation forward.

~~~

About Ben Carson

Dr. Carson is an emeritus professor of neurosurgery, oncology, plastic surgery and pediatrics at the Johns Hopkins School of Medicine. In 1984, he was named director of pediatric neurosurgery at Johns Hopkins Children's Center, a position he retired from on June 30, 2013. In 2008, he was named the inaugural recipient of a professorship in his name, the Benjamin S. Carson Sr., M.D., and Dr. Evelyn Spiro, R.N., Professor of Pediatric Neurosurgery. Also in 2008, he was awarded the Presidential Medal of Freedom, the highest civilian honor in the land.

Dr. Carson is interested in all aspects of pediatric neurosurgery and has a special interest in trigeminal neuralgia in adults. Through his philanthropic foundation, Carson Scholars Fund, he also is interested in maximizing the intellectual potential of every child. An internationally renowned physician, Dr. Carson has authored more than 100 neurosurgical publications and has been awarded more than 60 honorary doctorate degrees and dozens of national merit citations.

Dr. Carson writes a weekly syndicated column and has written five best-selling books. His fifth book, "America The Beautiful," was released early in 2012 and made The New York Times bestseller list.

~~~

Made in the USA
San Bernardino, CA
04 December 2015